Quest
for
PRESENCE

BOOK 1

THE MAP AND RADIANT FORCES

Joel B. Bennett, PhD

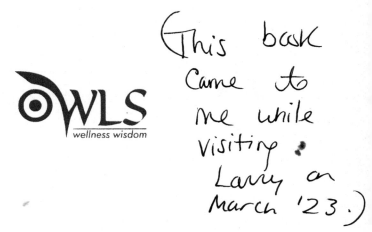

OWLS
wellness wisdom

This book
came to
me while
visiting :
Larry on
March '23.)

QUEST FOR PRESENCE MANDALA

The Radiant Forces

| Form | Chaos | Nurturing Conditions | Time Shaping |

The Soulful Capacities

| Acceptance | Presence | Flow | Synchronicity |

The Attractions

Crafting Potentiating Discerning Centering Synthesizing Coordinating Intending Catalyzing Opening

The Trajectories

Transcendence ———  ——— Interruption

Rhythm ——— ——— Pacing

Timing ——— ——— Routine

Transition ——— ——— Scheduling

The Treasures

Start here and flow clockwise →

← Spontaneity → Momentousness → Fulfillment → Clutch →
Optimism → Effortlessness → Ordinariness → Coherence →
Adoration → Resonance → Patience → Preciousness →
Savoring → Poignance → Release → Awe → Spontaneity →

Published by
Organizational Wellness and Learning Systems
FLOWER MOUND, TX

Editing by Candace Johnson, Change It Up Editing, Inc.; and
Sue Hansen, Duck Sauce Life, Inc.

Cover & interior by Gary A. Rosenberg • www.thebookcouple.com
Mandala art by author, Jeffrey McQuirk, and Rob Supan

Time, then, and the heaven came into being at the same instant in order that, having been created together, if ever there was to be a dissolution of them, they might be dissolved together.

—PLATO (FROM THE TIMAEUS)

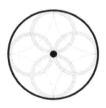

Quest for Presence Collection

The Connoisseur of Time: An Invitation to Presence

BOOK 1. The Map and Radiant Forces

BOOK 2. The Soulful Capacities

BOOK 3. The Attractions

BOOK 4. The Trajectories

BOOK 5. The Treasures and Destiny

Quest for Presence: Contemplations Workbook

For your precious journey . . .

Contents

Part Two. Four Radiant Forces

Author Note

Quest for Presence, or QfP for short, includes five books. Each can be read independently or as part of the whole; they need not be read in sequence. If you are just entering the collection, welcome! Your journey begins with *QfP Book 1: The Map and Radiant Forces.*

QfP is written and structured to support your sense that the particular book you are reading is just right for you. Indeed, the notion of time in QfP is about being wherever you happen to be.

Readers of QfP like that it has a "choose your own adventure" quality, offering a variety of entry points for engaging with core concepts. If you are new to these topics, I recommend that you read straight through each book. Please pause to review the contemplations at the end of most chapters (or complete corresponding activities in the QfP *Contemplations Workbook*, or both). It will help to read my personal reflections, as they illustrate how these concepts render in real life.

Each book also comes with notes in a research notes section, many of which relate to the science of time or provide references for readers interested in the related concept in the text. QfP is informed by a vast literature in the growing study and philosophy of time. However, these books are not intended to be evidence-based or academic. I am not summoning research to advance a new science of presence. I hope you will explore these notes only when your curiosity outweighs your desire to achieve time competency.

By time competency, I mean the ability to return to living in the present moment of your whole life (staying "on script," as it were).

There are two steps to being time competent. First, you notice when anxiety, worry, longing, or overthinking (your mental future) pull you away from the adventure; or when regret, remorse, self-judgment, or ruminations (your mental past) push you out of the moment. Second, you gently return to the here and now and the feeling that your whole-time is a happening, unfolding, or awesome life journey.

If you are re-entering the collection by way of another starting point, I invite you to reconnect to your journey. As is the nature of any quest, wherever you are along your path—and whichever book you find yourself reading—there you are.

The title of this book changed often as it went into final edits. This dynamic is a contemplation in itself. Does the way a book appears—judging a book by its title—make any difference to how you arrived here? I have listed the titles below. I think they all work. But the world requires us to fix things into a lasting word or image. I hope you find one that resonates with you.

A Quest for Presence, This Happening Life, Time's Precious Weave, Your Journey of Wholeness, Finding Free Time This Whole Time, Recovering Time in a World Addicted to Distraction and *Contemplations for Your Whole Time Here.*

* * *

I encourage you to download a free copy of the preview to QƒP on our website www.presencequest.life. *The Connoisseur of Time: An Invitation to Presence* has helped many get a solid grasp of the reason for this journey. You will also find resources and events on our site to support you in your quest.

ABOUT THE ABBREVIATION Q*f*P

The *f* symbol between Q and P (a letter f with a descender hook) is the notation used in mathematics to represent functions. Specifically, functions represent how a varying quantity depends on another quantity. For example, the position of a planet is a function of time, or a weekly salary is a function of the hourly pay rate and the number of hours worked, or supply is a function of demand: As price goes up, demand goes down. In our quest for presence, our journey is a function of our presence, and at the same time, our presence is a function of our journey. As you become more present, the experience of life as a happening adventure and unfoldment is more enhanced. As your experience of life enhances, you become more present. The thrill is in the ride, and the ride is in the thrill.

Introduction to All Books

To be present means to be present to the whole-time of your life. Being here now is important. Equally important is your whole life—where you came from and where you are headed. We just don't live in the now. Our whole life is a project of purpose and meaning, a coming into being, a path of sense-making, a place where everything fits together, a journey, a becoming, an arrival, a fulfillment of destiny, a momentous emergence, a cause, a calling, an awakening, and so much more. And all of these occur outside of "clock-time."

Presence happens when we show up and fully engage in this life with all its changes, interruptions, and distractions. Our presence is imperfect. I encourage you to embrace its imperfections. Our attention faces many challenges: advertisements, attention deficit, abuse, anxiety, aging, and cognitive decline, to name a few. Life is fleeting, a blur. How can you find the time to live it and live it well? Perhaps it's time to embrace the blur of your whole-time here.

This Quest for Presence (QfP) collection is designed to help you reach any number of objectives. This includes the actual letting go of specific deadlines in favor of contemplations that improve your presence. This idea may seem radical in a society oriented toward action, achievement, and accomplishment. As you will discover, this orientation is born out of a narrow-minded, fragmenting, and dysfunctional view that time comprises only "clock-time." A different, contemplative objective would be that you stop long enough to enjoy the rich, full, and precious aspects of this very brief life.

QƒP is about making room for uplifts, for positive moments, for glimpses of the amazing wonders and emotions that life has to offer. I call these *Treasures*. I hope you will become more curious about these Treasures. Where do they come from? How can you experience them more frequently? Through QƒP, I believe you will get answers to these questions. Your view of time will change. You will have more well-being, wholeness, and intimacy in your life—both with others and with the ever-evolving natural world.

Other objectives stem from these questions. A new perspective may help you be more efficient. To value your time in a new way may give you the motivation and tools to prioritize what matters most. As you discover the big picture of time, you may grow in your sense of spirituality, faith, and transcendence of life's problems. My personal aim for you lies in between these two areas: efficiency and spirituality. You embrace the ordinariness of life by becoming present to it.

Whatever your troubles, a shared presence can also make you resilient and thrive. This quest for presence is meant to be shared. We have arrived here as conscious beings because of cosmic forces that modern physics has only begun to understand. Deterioration of intimacy is the greatest problem of time compression (see my book *Time and Intimacy: A New Science of Personal Relationships* [Erlbaum, 2000]). We cannot appreciate our time without each other. As such, this offering is also a memoir. I hope you get to know me well enough so you feel less alone and more connected. And since we are here, we might as well make the most of it. Together.

Introduction to Book 1

B ook 1 of Quest for Presence (Q*f*P) is written in two parts.
Part One, "Time's Precious Tapestry," provides an overview or map for all five books, which correspond to five fundamental features of the tapestry:

+ four Radiant Forces
+ sixteen Treasures
+ four Soulful Capacities
+ eight Trajectories
+ nine Attractions

These features are ever- and dynamically interacting with each other, fading in and out, like threads in a precious weave.

Chapter 1 provides a "starter kit" with self-assessment exercises to help you dive right in and get familiar with these five features. I believe you will find it helpful to know how my purpose in writing Q*f*P—to improve your well-being and wholeness—unfolded over time. My career's focus, helping others practice well-being, has brought many opportunities to work with a wide variety of people from all walks of life.

Chapter 2 tells five stories showing how people do not have a healthy, empowered relationship with time and also how they can begin to do so with a new language of time.

Chapter 3 returns to the precious weave metaphor and revisits the five different features in more depth to give you a big-picture sense of them. Time is presented as a multilayered tapestry. Chapter 3 builds a graphic picture to help readers grasp the total framework of the entire Q*f*P collection. Of all the features in this framework, it is often the treasures or positive uplifts of life that help us embrace time in a new way.

Chapter 4 revisits the Treasures with real-life "treasure stories" I have collected from others. Chapter 4 functions as a preview of Book 5 in Q*f*P. Having developed a frame for viewing time in the previous chapters, chapter 5 suggests the best attitude for holding that frame. This final chapter in part one takes all the preceding ideas together and suggests readers can adjust their attitude toward time with specific steps, what I call the *Time Adjustment Protocol.*

Part Two is devoted to understanding the most abstract of all the features in the tapestry: the Radiant Forces. Understanding these forces is supported by four key insights described in successive chapters. The forces make up a totality or completeness of reality and nature (chapter 6). They hold everything together and create our experience of being held (chapter 7) and also of life's process and of life unfolding (chapter 8). They are the basis of seeing patterns in life and in cultivating wisdom (chapter 9). When we glimpse the totality, feel held, witness unfolding, or see patterns, we start to discern the operation of the forces in our lives (chapter 10).

Many readers will be well-oriented on their new journey, their presence quest, after reading this first book in its entirety. However, you can just complete the "starter kit" in chapter 1 and let the ideas and insights sink in. Alternately, feel free to skip ahead and browse through the Odes that begin, or the Contemplations that end, each chapter. Mostly, I encourage you to experiment by traveling different paths at different times. Honor your own process. Find your unique way of engaging with the Map and the Radiant Forces. You may be surprised. The precious weave will reveal itself to you as it guides your awakening.

PART ONE

Time's Precious Tapestry

Ode to Time: Waves

We were not born for the calendar
The days of our lives are not a set of tiles
   or checkerboard we hop upon

Instead, imagine a weaved pattern—
   threaded events going this way and that
memories … insights … longings

Or … even better … imagine this quilt bending
   and twisting in the wind of some destiny that
   blows through and escapes you

No, not even that

We are waves here
Rising and falling together
In a moment full and peaked
In a moment gone
In a moment merged
Catching light as we go

                     ~Joel B. Bennett (J.B.)

Life is precious. This is perhaps the most basic and greatest of all truths. We can know this truth each day, this day, your day. We have been taught a concept of time, clock-time, which obscures a more enriched view of time. "I am too busy to talk right now," "I don't have enough time," "We just have too many deadlines," or "I am so distracted with my phone, emails, and going back and forth. Ugh! ... zone out, tune out, burnout!"

It does not have to be this way. If we truly grasped that time compression is at the root of many personal and social problems, we would start an all-out effort to develop a new approach. We would get together to build a more liberating and inspiring view, a new language, of time. Research suggests that a sense of time urgency is a cause of cardiovascular risk or heart attacks, and that compressed and heavy workloads predict depression, anxiety, and burnout.* What we label as "stress" is a disguise for not slowing down to take that _precious moment to reorient to what is actually happening_ in this short life of ours.

May your own quest for presence represent an all-out effort. Let's reinvigorate our view of time as a set of Treasures that make life more purposeful, meaningful, and joyful. I want to reorient you to the vast array of inspiring yet fleeting Treasures that abound in every day of your life. Life not only happens _to_ you; it also happens _with_ you, and you _happen_ to life. When we fully grasp this, as individuals, as societies, as a planet, there will be less fragmentation in the world and more health and wholeness.

---

* This is the first of several dozen research notes that you will find referenced beginning on page 147. Other readers of this book suggested wanting these notes in the back of the book for easy reference but did not want to be interrupted by a citation note. From this point forward, I will not identify each research note and you can certainly go to the Research Notes section anytime.

CHAPTER 1

Starting Threads

REFLECTION

I reflect on the starting point of my journey through time. Two memories, time traces, follow. In the first, I am nine to twelve months old, lying on a diaper-changing table. Golden morning light pours in slants through venetian blinds. Two women, my mother and grandmother, are dressing me, cooing and smiling. The light has a soft, gauze-like quality that I reach out to touch. This light mingles with my caregivers' laughter and smiles and my giggles, in what I have come to know as adoration. All bundled together: light wafting like gauze, adoration, giggling. There was no sense of time, neither then nor in my memory now. Everything is suspended in Now space, just floating.

In the next memory, I am five or six years old. I wake up at night and stare into the darkness. I am deeply aware of my body, the entire sensation of being *inside* my body. I see my hands and hold them up to my face with a sense of cold finiteness. I know that my body, the skin that surrounds me, ends. My body separates from the rest of the world around me. It has a definite, stark, and clear end. I have the thought, "I will die. I will no longer be." Although difficult to convey, I am still able, with little effort, to re-create this feeling at will. Essentially, it is a mix of profound awe, terror, detachment, and also sadness at perceiving a deep and infinite nothingness, complete and cold void. I will not be. This body will no longer exist. Time (my time) is running out.

I run out of my bedroom to my parents. I wake them up, crying out, "I don't want to die!" They sit up and tell me to go back to sleep, with the insistence, "A child of your age should not be thinking about such things." They could have said everyone dies; that is just the way it is. Instead, "You're too young to think about it. Go back to sleep."

These memories of golden, warm adoration and cold, profound awe go as far back as my consciousness allows. They reflect two complementary strands, like those of every woven DNA molecule. And like DNA, they offer a set of instructions: I can experience the floating timelessness *within* this happening life as well as the void *beyond* it; I can immerse myself *in* life and detach *from* life; I can adore what life has to offer, and I can also go back to sleep. My life unfolds between the inspiring extraordinariness of *now* and the blank finality of biological time.

You are about to embark on a sort of treasure hunt. Treasure hunt journeys often involve finding something in the world: buried treasure, the Fountain of Youth, the Jade Temple, the Golden Fleece, or the Holy Grail. There is something *out there*, past the horizon, into the unknown future, that you need to—you must—get to. The current journey is different in three important respects: The treasure is found *in time* and not in space; it lies within the *now of your happening life* and not in the future; and it is an internal journey. In addition, the pace is more relaxed, much less urgent than a hunt. In short, you are about to learn a whole new language of time or, perhaps, a new language of whole-time. Either way, let's begin.

Almost all treasure stories begin with a map. Sometimes, a chance messenger tells you about a map hidden in some attic. Other times, you stumble upon a worn parchment: at the bottom of an old piece of luggage, inside a vase, or stuck in the fading pages of an old book. It will help for you to imagine that this chance, this stumble, is happening right now. Q*f*P is the harbinger of your treasure journey.

Since our treasure exists in time, the one-dimensional pages of a book do not contain it well. It may help to visualize the map as a continuous, ongoing weaving or tapestry of threads rather than a single sheet of paper. The following pages introduce this weave. As you continue, you will see it more as a multilayered mandala, a geometric configuration of meaningful symbols within your life.

I want to make something clear. I am not a keeper of any treasure. Only through chance and stumbling mentioned above have I found this path. It is best to think of me as a fellow journeyer rather than a guide. Please experiment with this time map just as you would explore any highways or trails marked on a map. I offer tools that have been helpful to me. The finding is within you.

The Precious Weave

What is the meaning of *precious weave*? As a noun, *precious* means something of great value (priceless, irreplaceable) that is not to be wasted or treated carelessly. As an adjective, it is a term of endearment or regard for some object, person, or living thing that one considers beloved. The word *weave* as a verb means to create a pattern (a fabric or story) by interlacing threads or elements together. It is also a noun, the accumulating form of the act of weaving: an interlacing, a knit, a braid, a twine, lattice work, a tapestry.

This precious weave, then, is your one valuable and currently happening life. It is an ever-forming tapestry, an unfolding story. Just as an author weaves a tale and the twists and turns of a plot unfold, your life is an unfolding of many precious moments and occasions. Recall my memories from above. We can immerse ourselves within life, or we can hurry through it, too anxious to notice. Within QfP, you will learn how to take the time to see, and you will learn about the nature of time itself.

This is where a treasure map can come in handy. I offer a starter kit of tools that you can use along the way. Let's begin with a series of self-reflection exercises, a sort of do-it-yourself introduction to the precious weave: the unfolding story of your happening life.

Your Starter Kit to the Q𝑓P Journey

Q𝑓P is devoted to understanding the unfolding map, the tapestry, the mandala. There are five tools in the Q𝑓P starter kit, each of which points to a different aspect of the tapestry. Each tool is discussed in much more detail in subsequent books. The Q𝑓P workbook contains more detailed versions of the self-reflection exercises outlined below.

Here are the five tools, or aspects of the tapestry, in your Q𝑓P starter kit: the *Radiant Forces* that weave, the *Soulful Capacities* you use to experience these forces, the *Attractions* you have toward these forces, the *Treasures* that emerge when our soul experiences the unfolding, and the *Daily Trajectories* (our comings and goings) in this happening life.

The sequence of the five sections presented below, starting with the Forces and ending with the Trajectories, is somewhat arbitrary. In our new time language, sequence is certainly a feature to contemplate, but not necessarily the most important. We take the sequence of "Past, Present, and Future" as monolithic, etched forever in stone. However, our experience of time need not be so sequential. For the five areas below (and the books they represent), please read them in any order that suits your intuition and inclination. If you have read this far, you probably have some calling to play with time anyway.

The Four Radiant Forces

The Treasures of this life are like a string of "now" pearls or "now" gems or "now" glowing beads of light. They are the everyday occurrences that happen before our eyes, and when we are present to them, they awaken us to wholeness. The four Radiant Forces help to create the Treasures, give you the consciousness to know them, and coax you to get up and dance with life. These forces work at the deepest level. They are the fundamental raw energy of the entire universe, the ever-present and bubbling constituents of every moment of your life.

Your life itself is an unfolding of beautiful Radiant Forces inviting you to dance, giving you the energy to bop, twirl, or chassé, all the while playing music in the background. Every occasion becomes a step in that dance. Every moment that you glimpse a Treasure and all the moments in between, the Treasures are incubating, percolating, bumping into each other. The Radiant Forces conspire to bring about your experience of this happening life. The four Radiant Forces are Time Shaping, Form, Nurturing Conditions, and Chaos. To begin to glean which of the Radiant Forces may be most prominent in your life right now, consider the four statements below. Select the one that best describes what is happening in your own particular life situation today.

✦ My life is well organized and relatively stable. I have a set of routines and can easily schedule things.

✦ My life is a mix of uncertainty, wonder, and things that I have to let go of. New things are happening, and I am changing.

✦ As I go about my day, I find it is better to allow things to unfold and see how things follow one after another. Everything in its own time.

✦ Every moment counts, and I tend to take advantage of the situation I am in. The world is what I make it.

If you selected the first statement, your life may be most governed by the Radiant Force of *Form*, the dance of gravity, and other universal constants that give a pattern to our lives. The artist has her tools, the hiker his equipment, and the scientist her systematic method. Life gives us these and other forms so we can navigate it, recognize patterns, and also use all its many features to make the most of our time here.

The second choice, about change, uncertainty, novelty, wonder, shows you the force of *Chaos* and the dance of entropy. Entropy is the degree of disorder or randomness in our universe. The artist, hiker, and scientist all deal with the unknown and chaotic world. Our vocation, our journey, may be defined by how we embrace this force.

If you selected the third item, your life may be most attuned to *Nurturing Conditions*, the facilitation of growth and becoming, the vital context from which all things arise. It is through the Nurturing Conditions of your life that you see the big picture, the meaning, the natural course of things.

The fourth force, *Time Shaping*, reveals the law of cause and effect or karma. By selecting this, you see yourself as a central actor within life. Your actions are part of a chain of events that never end. You tap this force to make a difference. The artist creates and designs. The journeyer takes steps. The scientist experiments.

These Radiant Forces constantly pull and move; they weave the threaded occasions of our life: the force of Form, of structure, of things holding together *in* time; the force of Chaos, of disintegration, of things dissipating *over* time; the force of Nurturing (or facilitating) Conditions, of things becoming, growing, and being *with* time; and the force of Time Shaping, of activity, taking action, of cause and effect *through* time.

The universe, the dance of these Radiant Forces, exists before and after you. Every human being navigates, dances, and experiences these forces in different ways. How, as well as how deeply, you experience them and this happening life is a result of inner workings deep within your being. Inside of you lie amazing capacities to experience the Treasures and the four forces. In fact, the Treasures of this happening life are the children of two parents: the universal Radiant Forces and your own unique soul.

The Four Soulful Capacities

Each of us has Soulful Capacities that we can cultivate, like a skill or a talent, to better experience all that life has to offer. Indeed, it is the very challenges, the stressors, the adversities of living that call us to cultivate these capacities. The Soulful Capacities represent your next set of tools in your QfP starter kit. In this brief exercise, take note of which are relatively strong or weak right now in your happening life.

	Doesn't Describe Me	Describes Me Very Little	Describes Me Some	Describes Me a Lot	Describes Me Greatly
1. I accept and approve of myself just as I am.	1	2	3	4	5
2. I easily forgive myself for mistakes I make.	1	2	3	4	5
Items 1 and 2 represent **Acceptance**	Total your scores (between 2 and 10): __10__				
3. I am calmly centered and present to life.	1	2	3	4	(5)
4. I cherish each moment of life.	1	2	3	4	(5)
Items 3 and 4 represent **Presence**	Total your scores (between 2 and 10): __10__				
5. I am easily flowing with changes in my life.	1	2	3	4	5 need to release mom
6. I find most chores and tasks easily rewarding.	1	2	3	4	(5)
Items 5 and 6 represent **Flow**	Total your scores (between 2 and 10): __9__				
7. I easily see the deep meaning of events. (100).	1	2	3	4	(5) ✗
8. I know I am in the right place and right time.	1	2	3	4	(5)
Items 7 and 8 represent **Synchronicity**	Total your scores (between 2 and 10): __11__				

These are the four Soulful Capacities. *Acceptance* includes a non-judgmental and open-minded quality. You see things as they are, being mindful, curious, and having a "one day at a time" attitude. *Presence* involves the ability to be fully attentive to oneself and one's environment, with a sense of aliveness, engagement, and tuning in to the moment with heart and mind. *Flow* is a state of being with a task or activity where one's sense of time disappears because one is so concentrated and in control, sometimes to the point of being in a state of grace. *Synchronicity* is often first understood as a meaningful coincidence and then as a knowing that everything happens for a reason that we can only glimpse. This insight that the universe is working behind the scenes is so radical that one feels that life is itself an occasion rich for discovery and perhaps a miracle.

As you reflect on these definitions and the ratings you made, what do you notice? If you judge or have negative thoughts about yourself for not having more of any of the specific capacities, then let that judgment go in Acceptance. If you have difficulty focusing, then in Presence, discover how to be with the distractions. If the exercise itself, this whole reading, is just dragging on or boring, then in Flow, realize a sense of energy from completing the task. If you feel pain or negative emotions or are having a hard time, then in Synchronicity, consider that miracles are about to happen in your life or that there is meaning to be discovered. This exercise is one step in untying the ribbon of a great gift. You are developing a set of competencies to help you live a better life by redefining your relationship with time.

To summarize, our soul, or essence, has four Soulful Capacities:

1. **Acceptance,** the ability to allow (not grasp or push away) anything in life that is disintegrating, forming, acting, or becoming;

2. **Presence,** the ability to show up and be fully in the moment;

3. **Flow,** the ability to continually move and adapt as things change; and

4. **Synchronicity,** the ability to see meaning as the forces and your soul coincide.

The Nine Attractions

You, like every other human being, are held together by the forces. You are woven by them. Your experience of this happening life arises as time unfolds in many distinct patterns. Your biological clock is ever-ticking; the traces of this life, your memories, are accumulating and mixing; the world, this living planet, is morphing; and you, your sense of self, is caught in a social web with its own rhythm of work, intimacy, play, and routine. Through these patterns, you have a personality, a wonderfully unique way of enfolding the forces into your own style of living.

Actually, you are attracted to different forces at different times. You also have a tendency to be drawn toward one more than another. There are nine Attractions that align with these tendencies. Review the following list and consider: *Which one most resonates with you? Which one do you think best describes you?*

1. **Catalyzing.** I like to initiate things, keep the spark going, and discover the next horizon, even to the point of challenging the routine and status quo.

2. **Intending.** I am a person of action, always want to seize the day and make things happen. If I have an intention to get something done, I typically follow through.

3. **Coordinating.** I enjoy engineering things or coordinating elements of a situation as efficiently as possible with an eye to how it will all turn out in the future.

4. **Centering.** I have an ongoing ability to remain poised or calm in most situations and bring that sense of centeredness, peace, and listening, allowing things to unfold in an organized way.

5. **Discerning.** I enjoy taking time with the details of a situation, diplomatically working with others to discern what will resonate with or work for as many as possible and for the greatest good.

6. **Potentiating.** I see the possibilities and potential of things and people; I love nurturing and cultivating the potential as much as I can to bring out the best in the situation.

7. **Crafting.** I am creative in almost every area of my life, enjoying the arts, drama, and music, and I immerse myself in any creative effort I take on.

8. **Opening.** I enjoy surprises, novelty, and pivoting, and I keep an open mind on this wondrous journey of life.

9. **Synthesizing.** I maintain a central viewpoint that brings together both taking action and taking time as well as seeing order in the chaos. I am an integrator.

These are the nine personality Attractions. It is all right if you select more than one right now. As we move forward, you will learn how to discern when you or others are engaging a particular attraction.

These Attractions are not fixed traits or types as much as things we like to do. We like to catalyze and challenge (question things, take risks), intend and time shape (activate, inspire action), coordinate (engineer things, calculate), center and organize (stabilize), discern and negotiate (take perspective, communicate), potentiate and nurture (help, cultivate, facilitate for others), craft (design, customize), open and innovate (create, try new things), and integrate (synthesize and unify).

To summarize, each of us has a set of tendencies toward the Radiant Forces. For example, perhaps most obviously, those attracted to Form will be drawn to center themselves or get centered and organize, whereas those attracted to Chaos will be more inclined toward openness and innovation. Other Attractions represent a dual focus. For example, coordinating and engineering things suggests an attraction to both Form and Time Shaping.

The Sixteen Treasures

The QfP starter kit includes a list of the Treasures themselves. These are like different colors for the artist, special vantage points on your journey, or the periodic table of elements for a chemist. The sixteen basic Treasures can be seen in nuanced ways, like a glint, or in their fullness, like a sudden jolt. (Note: To get started, we focus on these sixteen Treasures, but see the list at the back of this book for many more.)

Your next exercise is to review the list below. Rate each Treasure in terms of how likely you are to experience it within the next day. Imagine yourself experiencing these feelings, states, or events, and predict how likely they are to happen. Pay close attention to your feelings—your intra-sensory perception—as you make each rating. You may want to look at the clock right now for fun and come back in twenty-four hours to see if you were right!

How likely will you experience the state or event below in the next day?	Not At All Likely	Not Likely	Likely	Very Likely
1. Ordinariness. Just calmly being with what is; needing nothing special.	1	2	3	(4)
2. Coherence. Sensing harmony in your life; noticing how things fall into place; a previous confusion begins to make sense.	1	2	3	(4)
3. Adoration or Charm. A sense of softly holding an experience, person, or object; positive regard; being absorbed with or taken by something.	1	2	3	(4)
4. Harmony or Resonance. A sense of vibrating together between you and others; being in tune with whatever is happening; witnessing togetherness in a way that moves you.	1	2	3	(4)
5. Release. Any of the following: Letting go; detaching; surrendering; experiencing peace from resolving an issue; relief.	1	2	3	(4)

How likely will you experience the state or event below in the next day?	Not At All Likely	Not Likely	Likely	Very Likely
6. Awe/Humility. Feeling a sense of wonder or amazement; seeing your place in the grand scheme.	1	2	3	(4)
7. Spontaneity. Doing anything spontaneous; leaping into; suddenness; a joyful impulse; abandonment.	1	2	(3)	4
8. Momentousness. A sense of being at a tipping point; a jolt; initiation or beginning; conversion; awakening.	1	2	3	(4)
9. Patience. Allowing things to unfold at their own rate; a sense of ease. Doing things in moderation.	1	(2)	3	4
10. Preciousness. Cherishing the transitory moment; having a rich affection for life.	1	2	3	(4)
11. Savoring. Tasting the moment; reveling; relishing; delighting in the senses.	1	2	3	(4)
12. Poignance/Forgiveness. The quality of evoking a keen sense of sadness or regret; finding some interaction or event touching or deeply affecting; bittersweet; ironic. Releasing feelings of resentment.	1	2	3	(4)
13. Fulfillment. Sense of finally arriving; accomplishment; reaching a plateau; nirvana; satori.	1	2	3	(4)
14. Clutch (refers to "in a clutch" or a tight or critical situation). Performing under pressure; rising to the occasion; seizing the day; victory.	1	2	3	(4)
15. Optimism. Having a positive outlook; a move to thriving; overcoming; expecting goodness.	1	2	3	(4)
16. Effortlessness. Absence of strain; enjoying continuity; a simple, smooth, fluent action.	1	2	3	(4)

Let's pause for a moment to summarize. The Treasures help you experience the wonder and preciousness of this life. The Radiant Forces are the voice of the universe speaking into and through the Treasures. The Soulful Capacities are your ability to experience the Treasures. The Attractions reflect your tendencies, your personality, for enfolding the forces into your life.

Time also happens in the more mundane aspects—the situations—of daily living. Every day, as we traverse the map or watch the tapestry, our comings and goings reflect the operation of the Radiant Forces. They are the trajectories of living. While these forces work at the deepest level, daily life is where we are, where we spend our time "on the surface." The four Radiant Forces are always interacting with each other to bring about the different facets, or trajectories, of our daily life.

The Eight Trajectories

Nearly everything that happens in your day is a function of one of the eight Trajectories: *Routine, Scheduling, Transition, Timing, Rhythm, Transcendence, Interruption,* and *Pacing.* The last exercise brings us back into your day-to-day experience of time; how time unfolds in the flow of life, your own trajectory, the path of your day. What did you do today? As you read the description of each trajectory, notice where you have spent most of your attention recently. Rate how much attention you have given to each of the following areas.

As I reflect on my attention to time in the past day, I find that ...	Not at all	Sometimes	Often	Frequently
1. I do the same things as usual, experience repetition, similar work, with regularity or rituals, and keep events in order. (**Routine**)	☐	☐	☐	☒

As I reflect on my attention to time in the past day, I find that ...	Not at all	Sometimes	Often	Frequently
2. I spend time prioritizing; I focus on upcoming events, plan, work with to-do lists, calendars, and find time for things that need getting done. (*Scheduling*)	☐	☐	☐	☒
3. I attend to or am caught up in some transition either in my life or in someone close to me, some phase in my life (project, work, family) that is either ending or beginning. (*Transition*)	☐	☐	☒	☐
4. I make efforts to find the right time for things; time to communicate, be effective, find a right match, coordinate, come, go, take action, or just do nothing. (*Timing*)	☐	☐	☐	☒
5. I attend to or enjoy natural rhythms for myself (such as sleep, wake, work) and with others (come, meet, leave) so that things are synchronized and not frenetic. (*Rhythm*)	☐	☐	☐	☒
6. I discover time outside of time where I am not caught up in any of the other trajectories; I relax and let things unfold. (*Transcendence*)	☐	☐	☒	☐
7. My day is filled with interruptions or unforeseen events that take up my time in ways that I had not planned. (*Interruption*)	☒	☐	☐	☐
8. My day has a relatively even or steady pace within different events and from one event to another. (*Pacing*)	☐	☐	☒	☐

As you reflect on your responses, note that every day is likely different from the next. The key here, as with all the exercises, is to refrain from judgment. Just observe. You are starting to develop a new language of time.

Every day, we have the opportunity to transcend clock-time, to glimpse the Radiant Forces, experience the Treasures, observe the Attractions in ourselves and others, and nurture our Soulful Capacities.

So congratulations. You have completed your Quest for Presence starter kit. Imagine waking up every day with an eye toward finding the Treasures. Doing so automatically changes your attitude toward time. Time does not happen to you as much as life becomes a journey that includes time: your friend who, in a curious but loyal way, has been with you *the whole time*.

an eye toward finding the treasures.

Contemplations

At the end of every chapter, you will find an opportunity to contemplate, journal, or discuss ideas. The Q*f*P workbook is provided as an additional tool. The workbook goes into more depth for each contemplation and gives you space for journaling. For this first contemplation, pause for a moment and reflect on the five elements of the self-reflection exercises: the four Radiant Forces, the four Soulful Capacities, the nine Attractions, the sixteen Treasures, and the eight Trajectories.

Contemplation (Qƒp 1-1)*:
Reflect on the Big Picture

As you reflect, how would you answer these questions?

✦ Review each of the five quick self-assessments in this chapter (the four Radiant Forces, the four Soulful Capacities, etc.). Which of these piqued your interest? What intuitions do you have about how each relates to the others?

✦ Within your daily life, how much time do you spend either contemplating or being aware of each of these five elements? How much time would you like to spend?

✦ What do you see as the "big picture" of these areas? What best describes your perception: Overwhelmed or spacious? Contracted or expanded? Closed or open? Chaotic or organized? Complex or simple?

✦ Review the image of each of the words below. Imagine that they make up a new language of time. Imagine that, from the present moment forward, you never use the word "time" again in your life. Instead, you unpack what is really happening. You dig deeper. The words are placed in random order below and with different sizes and shading. It is an example, a moment captured in the quest. This is to represent that at any given moment of your precious consciousness, some features come into the foreground while others fade. There is a continuous emergence of radiance in your quest. So, right now, what are you noticing. What is moving into the foreground? What is shifting? Ultimately, what is happening?

---

* Each contemplation in all of the books in QƒP is also found in the workbook. To help find these, we use the notation of QƒP #-# to designate the book in the collection and the Contemplation within that book. Hence, this first Contemplation QƒP 1-1 is the first Contemplation in Book 1.

release

PRESENCE

resonance

Scheduling

spontaneity preciousness

coherence **Interruption** Transcendence

TIME SHAPING NURTURING CONDITIONS

optimism

forgiveness

Rhythm

Routine

CHAOS

clutch

momentousness

Timing

FLOW patience

harmony **ACCEPTANCE**

adoration

awe TRANSITION

savoring

FORM poignance **Pacing**

SYNCHRONICITY

charm **ordinariness** fulfillment

effortlessness

w/ choir solo + musical

CHAPTER 2

Impact on Our Well-Being

Ode to Stories

We are ever breathing churning stories.
Even while we sleep.

Don't just say: "We are our stories."
How trite, metaphoric, academic!

You are
either bloody into the whole damn thing
or
You are
Not.

~ J.B.

M any of us have been raised in a culture that values primarily one type of time: the quantity of labor from clock-time. These social norms impact our health, our sleep, our recovery from strain, our poor use of leisure, and our turning to addictive gadgetry for temporary (rather than deep) relief. Those with power and money dictate this corporate orientation to time because it brings them more power and money. It is truly _time_ to find, create, or experiment with more innovative and "stealth" strategies to empower ourselves. QfP is designed to empower, to help you be an entrepreneur with your time.

Become an
entrepreneur of
your time

Many problems can be traced to having a poor relationship to time. For example, we tend to focus more on how much work we can accomplish (what Martin Hägglund calls "labor time") rather than improving the quality of how we spend our free time. We also spend more time offering opinions about what is right or wrong (judging, criticizing, polarizing) than we do simply being in one another's presence. Consider how our relationship with time creates the following problems:

+ Time pressure leads to stress, poor health, and heart disease.

+ A fast-paced, 24/7 work environment can foster loneliness, alienation, and even depression.

+ Fast or processed and ultra-processed foods promote time pressure to consume and also lack nutrients that can promote longer and healthier time for digestion and absorption into the body.

+ We have less time on weekends for our bodies and minds to unwind and recover.

+ Rapid-fire and bite-size social media posts (mindless tweets or senseless criticisms) damage relationships.

+ We are more likely to believe in false information—and experience negative emotions—when under time pressure to consume data (scrolling through social media posts) than when we take the time to deliberate about information.

+ "Quick-fix," addictive smartphone apps and tools jolt the fight-flight mechanisms in our brains and cause stress.

These problems are based on clock-time: the sense, drilled into us as children, that time moves in a straight line in chunks of seconds, minutes, weeks, years. The digitization of linear time has led to many advances in engineering, technology, and computer systems. With quantum computing and artificial intelligence, more advances are on the way. But, as the list above shows, these innovations have a cost. New gadgets and tools appear to create more disposable time. How can we apply this time to <u>enhance our quality of life</u> rather than using gadgets as a <u>mindless distraction</u>?

I believe the answer requires having a new, empowered view and language of time. This language can bring more consciousness, connection, and wholeness. I have personally used this new language in all areas of my life to great benefit. I use it at home, with coworkers, with clients, and when I teach.

> *"The real measure of value is not how much work we have done or have to do (quantity of labor time) but how much disposable time we have to pursue and explore what matters to us (<u>quality of free time</u>)."*
>
> *~ Martin Hägglund, modern philosopher*

Our systemic adherence to clock-time (small "t" time) prevents us from experiencing the benefits of life: our health, well-being, and happiness. Over the past thirty years, I have often asked people why they don't take Time (big "T" time) out for health, spirituality, or to de-stress. They most commonly say they do not have enough time. Their comments are supported by studies on burnout in the helping professions. When I ask those responsible for the health or well-being of others—doctors, teachers, therapists, healthcare or wellness professionals—why they don't pause for their own well-being, they say, "I am just too busy." (Paradox ... laugh out loud!)

Moments of Coherence about Time

Five experiences stand out as *aha* moments (**Momentousness**) in my own journey to better understand time. I share them in the hope that they will help you reflect on your own "why" for taking this Quest for Presence journey. (Note: In this section, I will use some of the words and phrases that make up the Q*f*P's new language about time. These will be in the text in **bold italics**. In later chapters and in other books in the collection, I expand on these definitions so you will be better equipped to apply them in your life).

The Head Nurses

In one of my first professional workshops in the 1980s, I delivered time-management training for head nurses at a busy city hospital. I began by asking open-ended questions and listening to the responses. It became clear that these nurses, all women, were what I might call "time adepts"; they were aces in managing clock-time and arranging schedules with keen foresight. They shouldered enormous responsibility of managing these routines amid a constant background of emergencies, employee turnover, difficult physicians, and continuous changes in administration, policy, and technology. They weathered all of this because they exemplified the force of **Nurturing Conditions**. Their hearts were deeply in their work. They valued life, and they derived deep enjoyment from serving others.

It is not easy being a head nurse. These women, most in their forties and fifties, found ways of side-stepping the work pressures. But too much side-stepping comes at a cost. All were overweight; many complained about pain, compassion fatigue, exhaustion, or burnout. In response, we worked on how they could give themselves more time, set self-care priorities, and find ways of pacing themselves (**Pacing**). We spent time helping them acknowledge each other and the different gifts they brought by working as a team.

In other words, the workshop became a "time out of or away from time." It was more a retreat to savor time together than a training on skills that would be a challenge for them to employ (**Savoring**). I learned then that it was more important to help them practice *presence* with each other and enjoy their break (**Presence**) rather than teach them about things they already knew but were not able or willing to practice, especially given the time demands of their workplace.

The Medical Directors

Another aha experience came in the 1990s. Serving in an advisory role, I had an opportunity to dialogue with medical directors for some of the largest corporations in the United States. They shared that employee stress was the greatest driver (cause) of medical costs

Time away from time

in their companies (this is still true today, twenty-five years later). I asked them whether they would be willing to implement effective stress-management tools, tools known to lessen stress and reduce the rising medical costs hurting their companies. These medical directors were thoughtful, expressing interest in the techniques, but reported they simply did not have the time in their *schedules* to implement the techniques (*Scheduling*). Work operations did not permit the dissemination of evidence-based tools.

Essentially, they were communicating that their workers are responsible for dealing with stress in their own time (and away from work). The underlying—and mistaken—belief is that we are all in charge of how we use and shape time. We suffer from the delusion that each of us is our own time shaper, someone who operates in a vacuum. This belief, and the continued lack of response of employers to the growing stress crisis, makes no logical sense to me. It was not *coherent* to me from a health perspective (*Coherence*). Why continue to neglect something that causes illness? The answer to this question insinuates a root cause to most problems in work stress. Namely, the operations or work system of a company that creates time pressures, the very thing that causes strain, is also related to the company's ability to be successful.

This is often called a "double bind," a situation with two competing and irreconcilable demands. The choices are to either: (A) slow down or stop production as a way to encourage workers to be healthier and more productive in the long run, potentially losing money in the process; or (B) keep producing to make money in the short run. Option B contains the risk of wearing employees down, causing strain and disease, which ultimately results in lower productivity and higher medical costs. The short-sightedness of option B is a recipe for an unending cycle of negative financial returns due to health problems.

My conversation with these doctors occurred more than twenty years ago. We now know with certainty that the costs of stress due to poor corporate stewardship of health are massive and out of control.

They cost US employers more than $300 billion annually and cause an estimated 120,000 excess deaths each year (see Jeffrey Pfeffer's 2018 book, *Dying for a Paycheck*). There are now many efforts and solutions to what I call the "time-stress problem." Things are improving. Recent research shows a significant increase in the use of on-site stress-management programs, more positive overall health outcomes among organizations that encourage stress management, and more organizations considering stress and resilience programs as "must-haves."

* * *

One lesson I gleaned from the medical directors all those years ago still applies today. People, often those with authority, cite a lack of time for not taking preventive action. They use the term "stress" (often unwittingly) as a cover-up for their own manipulative orientation to time. Stress is not our real problem; it is time. This sentence warrants repetition: Stress is not our real problem; it is time, at least the way we define it.

The Young Mother

My experience with the corporate doctors reminded me of an earlier experience while listening to an interview with anthropologist Edward T. Hall on Wisconsin Public Radio's *Wisconsin Talks*. I had previously read Hall's 1984 book *The Dance of Life: The Other Dimension of Time*, which influenced my own orientation to **this happening life**. In his book and the interview, Hall explained the difference between two types of cultures and *monochronic versus polychronic time*.

People in monochronic cultures tend to do one thing at a time and see time as made up of small parcels (digitized) that can be scheduled, arranged, and managed. People in polychronic cultures tend to do many things at once. They view time as more fluid, made up of larger sections, and they place more emphasis on relationships than on tasks or getting things done. Monochronic cultures emphasize *shaping time*: taking action, getting information, and realizing a goal (**Time Shaping**); whereas polychronic cultures see the Nurturing Conditions or context surrounding events and emphasize relationships, community, and the circumstances we live in.

My ears perked up when a woman, a new mother, called into the Hall interview. She was concerned about how she was raising her young child. She experienced her child as naturally, or innately, polychronic. She had her own **rhythms**, lived completely in a symbiotic relationship of mother-to-child, and followed routines that came organically more from the inside-biological world than the civilized, outside world (**Rhythms**). As I recall, this young mother was quite anxious about forcing her child (a round peg) into a clock-time system (a square hole) that she perceived as not healthy for the child.

Hall acknowledged the challenge this young mother faced. For me, it brought home the compromises we make from living in a consumer-oriented culture. It is no surprise that in the past twenty years, more and more of our culture has become push-button, immediate, and 24/7. Google, Facebook, Amazon, and YouTube give instant access to everything; this is a natural outcome of a monochronic culture. From this perspective, seeing the powerful and overarching force of culture, it makes perfect sense that the medical directors blamed the lack of time; it makes sense that the head nurses were overweight and burned out. These people are not wholly responsible for their own mindless actions toward time. To some extent, they are a product of a monochronic culture.

The Retreatant

A wellness or spiritual retreat provides a wonderful opportunity to review our actions toward time and make these actions more mindful. Several years back, I guided such a retreat. A few days before, I gave a talk at the local church that was to host the retreat. I talked about how time in our culture is like a treadmill that we need to take a break from, the importance of having intimacy with ourselves and our surroundings, and the need for taking time out of our busy lives.

After my talk, a woman came up to me and said she very much enjoyed what was shared, and she found it helpful. She explained that the *timing* was off for her to come to the retreat (**Timing**). She could have used my insights earlier in the busy time of her life, but not now that she was in her late middle-age and retired. I thanked her for her honesty and did not expect to see her again.

It was a surprise when she showed up at the retreat on the following Saturday (**Spontaneity**).

After the opening circle at this retreat, everyone completed a self-assessment and then went off to separate locations to do a journaling activity in privacy. This woman went to the pillow area, and there she stayed, napping for most of the rest of the day. I (and others) would check on her occasionally, and she seemed to be peaceful and calm in her quiet space. She joined us for the closing circle at the end of the day. When it was her turn to share, she indicated that she had spent her life being too busy and never giving herself permission to just rest. The space that the retreat provided allowed her to check in with herself for the first time in a long while. What she discovered was the need to rest and take an **ordinary** nap (**Ordinariness**). She became fully **present** to what she needed (**Presence**) and **released** older and self-imposed expectations about time (**Release**). I had been worried about her lying there all day; now, I envied her due to my own workaholism.

"Out beyond ideas of wrong-doing and right-doing there
is a field. I'll meet you there. When the soul lies down in
that grass the world is too full to talk about."
~ Mawlana Jalaluddin Muhammad Rumi, Sufi poet, mystic

For some context, here is how I facilitate this type of retreat. At the beginning of the day, all participants sit in a "meeting circle" and review the purpose of the retreat: to **transcend time** (**Transcendence**). Each person has an opportunity to share their story and what they hope to get out of the day. I explain that the retreat is for them to meet themselves in their own time. They should follow their own **pace** for the day as they feel so led (**Pacing**). I ask retreatants to come back to the circle at scheduled times. However, since they also are encouraged to find their own *rhythms*, they may continue with some personal activity (such as journaling, walking, noticing nature), and therefore, they do not have to promptly return to the group (**Rhythm**). I bring a set of pillows, cushions, and blankets to the retreat, inviting participants to take time to rest if that is what they need. You may benefit by approaching this QfP book collection with a similar attitude. Pace yourself as you feel led.

The Well-Being Champions

My company offers training and support for businesspeople responsible for helping coworkers use health promotion services. These people are called wellness coordinators, advocates, ambassadors, or champions. We have a book on the subject, *Well-Being Champions: A Competency-Based Guidebook*, which I coauthored with Dr. Brittany Linde. As part of our work, we surveyed champions to find out what they need and the barriers they face to engaging employees.

For one study, we asked about eighty champions from almost as many different businesses what prevented them from engaging employees in their wellness programs. The most frequently cited problem was "not enough time on my hands," with almost 80% of the respondents rating it as "somewhat of a problem" or "a big problem." Following close behind were "work stress/work overload" and "lack of budget," each of which was seen as a problem by almost 70% of respondents. Other barriers included "wellness not being a management priority" (60%), "lack of being prepared or trained as a champion" (50%), and "lack of materials/resources" (40%).

When our analysis looked at only these barriers, it was clear that time and stress were the biggest issues. No surprise there. However, when we looked at the data to determine what factors predicted success, we found that wellness champions who could "deliver time" to employees saw the highest program participation rates. That is, we looked at whether the business provided employees with access to health-producing activities (for example, having a wellness committee, hosting lunchtime learning sessions, sponsoring employee sports leagues, having an employee field day).

We also found that the actual barriers were less important than the respondents' perceptions, especially with respect to their *optimism* (*Optimism*), their belief in themselves, their perception of employee readiness to participate in programming, and the length of tenure in their role. In other words, while time and stress were perceived to be barriers, in reality, they were not barriers to taking action among more optimistic champions.

My work with wellness champions illustrates that time is what we make of it. We can either lament its lack, or we can empower ourselves to use what we have. Consider these two quotes: Winston Churchill said, "The pessimist sees difficulty in every opportunity; the optimist sees opportunity in every difficulty," and Greek Stoic philosopher Epictetus said, "The obstacle is the way."

* * *

These five experiences represent an evolution in my understanding of time, milestones on my journey. The nurses taught me that there is power in just taking time out to listen. A space for listening can itself provide a community some relief and *release* (*Release*), giving a chance to find values and feelings that *resonate* with them (*Resonance*) and are nourished in the process. The medical directors showed how the hard reality of the monochronic business world often puts decision-makers in a double bind. The challenge of balancing productivity against prevention and well-being is not an easy one.

The young mother who called into the Edward T. Hall interview taught me that most people, especially mothers, deeply know the health-producing and *precious* resource of biological, or organic, time (*Preciousness*). We can pay attention to our own inner *rhythms* and cycles (*Rhythm*). The woman retreatant showed me the importance of following this inner guidance system, especially when workaholism threatens our ability to be present to our happening life. Who would have thought that taking a nap was a brave thing to do? The wellness champions taught me that perspective or attitude is everything. We need to seize every opportunity to listen, balance priorities, and give ourselves and others the opportunity to *flow* with time, off the clock (*Flow*).

Contemplation (Q*f*P 1-2):
Reflect on Stories

The five stories represent different themes related to time. The themes of power, creativity, and empowerment connect the stories together. At a personal level, the mother and the retreatant made the decision to prioritize their *precious* time and *savor* life's gift. At a professional level, the head nurses, medical directors, and wellness champions all expressed a certain amount of powerlessness and frustration over the inflexibilities of *schedule* and *pace* imposed by the work culture. At the same time, depending on the scenario, there was an opportunity to be *present*, to plan, to *accept*, to reflect, to show *optimism*, and to get validation for feeling frustrated. The following questions can be used for journaling or discussion to help you dig deeper into these themes:

+ Which of the five stories did you most identify with? Why? Do you have a similar experience?

+ Which of the stories is most inspiring to you? Which story makes you want to take action? Why? How does it point to a growth opportunity for you?

+ How can a person or workplace be more empowered around their use of time? How can you empower yourself? What message can you find in these stories that helps with such empowerment?

+ Are we simply a product of living in a culture that blindly adheres to clock-time? Can we do anything about it? How much? How can we broaden our sense of time?

✦ What are some ways that you can be creative in your use of time? At home? At work?

Finally, think about your own story. Recall moments in your life where you either intuited, sensed, or realized that time, as defined by your education or culture, was wholly different than that definition. Recall the circumstance and what led you to that perception.

Time is not linear.
It does not chase me.
me, nor pull me.
It's simply a resume
" Spitted story" use

CHAPTER 3

A Map of
This Happening Life

Ode to Happening

Who knows what is really happening?

This is all an act, they say.
You search in the dark for the script.

This is a resting place for a longer journey, they say.
You search in the dawn light for a cup of coffee and
    maybe a newspaper to read.

Others claim you are ever arriving.
The sojourn is the pattern itself.
You are yourself worth the read.

~ J.B.

Here is the fundamental assumption of this book: **Life is happening!** A bunch of stuff is all happening at the same time. It is all a blur. Without consciousness and attention, it would be impossible to live. Tremendous changes in our world, society, and way of living add to the blur. You could go off the grid, join a retreat or pilgrimage. However, wherever you go, there you are. Life still happens. A guiding principle can help:

Life is Happening. The process of this happening
life may be complex, but finding purpose and
joy within it need not be complicated.

Since many things are going on at once, let's peel back some layers. What is the simplest approach, the fewest number of layers, needed to see the *process* of this happening life?

To answer this question, I borrow a metaphor that writers have used from time immemorial: Life is a journey.

Consider just these few:

Do your work, then step back. The only path to serenity.
~ LAO TZU (TAOIST SAGE)

In all your ways submit to the Lord, and
he will make your paths straight.
~ PROVERBS 3:6 (NIV)

God created humanity from a single soul, appointing
us this place to sojourn and to depart from. The
signposts are clear to those who study this life.
~ QUR'AN 6:98

To finish the moment, to find the journey's end in every step of
the road, to live the greatest number of good hours, is wisdom.
~ RALPH WALDO EMERSON (AMERICAN PHILOSOPHER)

A nomad I will remain for life. In love
with distant and uncharted places.
~ ISABELLE EBERHARDT (SWISS AUTHOR)

The journey is what brings us happiness
... not the destination.

~ Dan Millman (American author)

The key to realizing a dream is to focus not on success
but significance—and then even the small steps and little
victories along your path will take on greater meaning.

~ Oprah Winfrey (American entertainer and author)

These quotes may inspire us. At the same time, the journey metaphor is vague, lacking specific guidance.

If life is a journey, then where is the map? I could use some help here! In preparing this book, I wondered: Is it possible to furnish a new map that might apply practical wisdom from the above quotes and many other insights like them?

Two Perspectives on the Map

In the QfP starter kit in chapter 1, you reflected on all five aspects of the map, tapestry, or mandala. In this section, you will gain a clearer sense of this new map of your happening life. Because each of us has a different learning style, I seek to appeal to your own way of learning.

Some people learn through self-reflection, as offered in the QfP starter kit. Others learn through lists, sentences organized into clear objectives. Many people also appreciate guidance through visual images: diagrams, charts, or videos. Below, I present the map in two perspectives so that you can better appreciate how the five features interact to produce the blur of this happening life. Use whichever one suits you.

Perspective 1: The Map as a Course of Study

The map of this happening life can be summarized in eleven basic ideas. These ideas are organized below as a curriculum or course outline, with a purpose and objectives.

Purpose: Realize that you were sent here to discover the Treasures in your life that are accessible to you every day.

As a result of this study, you will be able to meet three objectives:

Objective 1. Understand that cosmic Radiant Forces make up everything that happens and that these forces also inform your soul.

Objective 2. Recognize how both your personality and the activities of your day-to-day existence provide opportunities to recognize and work with these forces.

Objective 3. Identify and experience the Treasures of this happening life.

Key Ideas

1. The map of this happening life is composed of threads that are woven together.

2. Each thread is a string or ribbon that moves in and through time.

3. Each string is made up of moments. These moments, banded together, are occasions.

4. These moments are the bridges (the connections) between very deep cosmic forces and all other elements on the map. They allow us to make connections, transcend, find meaning, and experience the real treasure of life.

5. There are four dynamic factors, cosmic Radiant Forces, that are constantly pulling and moving (weaving) these threads. These forces are:

   ✦ The force of Chaos, of disintegration, of things dissipating over time;

   ✦ The force of Form, structure, and pattern, of things holding together in time;

   ✦ The force of Time Shaping, of taking action, of cause and effect through time; and

✦ The force of Nurturing (or facilitating) Conditions, of things becoming, growing, and being with time.

6. Each of us has arrived for the journey. We wake up to this fact, and we navigate the map with both a soul and a personality.

7. Your soul, or essence, has capacities. These Soulful Capacities are:

✦ Acceptance, or the ability to allow (not grasp or push away), anything in your life that is disintegrating, forming, acting, or becoming;

✦ Presence, or the ability to show up and be fully in the moment;

✦ Flow, or the ability to continually move and adapt as things change; and

✦ Synchronicity, or the ability to see meaning (pattern) as or when the Radiant Forces and your soul coincide.

8. We each have a personality or Attractions, a set of preferences or tendencies toward the forces. These are not fixed traits or types as much as things we like to do. As reviewed earlier in chapter 1, we are drawn to certain activities over others. Each of us has proclivity for some things over others. We are more likely to move toward and engage in certain types of activities or experiences over other types of activities or experiences. We identify eight different Attractions. This means we are more likely to gravitate to situations where we get to either: catalyze and challenge, intend and shape time, coordinate and engineer, center and organize, discern and negotiate, potentiate and nurture, craft and design, create and innovate, or integrate and unify.

9. Your personality navigates the map on a day-to-day basis, whereas your soul uses the map on a long-term basis. Daily life makes up the surface of the map, whereas the forces make up the deeper weave and continually influence your daily life. Our souls know what our personalities only dimly perceive.

"our Soul knows what our personalities only dimly percieve."

10. Your attention to and sense of time emerges in your daily life through the interplay of the forces. There are eight different paths, or Trajectories, in your daily life: Routine, Scheduling, Transition, Timing, Rhythm, Transcendence, Interruption, and Pacing.

11. Every moment or occasion is an opportunity to find life's Treasures: those things that uplift or inspire us; bring us joy, meaning, understanding; and help us to see life as a gift.

These ideas are "the precious weave" of life. Alternatively, the map is *the* precious weave. I call the desire for the Treasures the "quest for presence." And, yes, presents are gifts as well. The more fully we understand the first ten ideas, the more likely we find, stumble upon, discover, explore, and help others with the Treasures.

Time Map, Brain Map

A map allows us to make the most of our time, our journey, and our location so we do not get lost. Assuming we know where we want to go, a map also saves us time by avoiding distractions. We can get our bearings, know where we are, where we came from, and where we are headed. Most important, a map helps us explore the unknown, make decisions, and find connections between places, layers, and levels in the terrain the map represents.

Before presenting a visual guide, I want to say a few things about the human brain, perhaps the greatest map that ever existed. There is a relationship between how we map time in this book and how scientists have been mapping the brain. This "Perspective 2" is, at a tacit or unconscious level, informed by my own early studies in brain research. Karl Pribram, one of the great neuroscientists of our time, wrote a great deal about how the brain self-organizes and functions like a hologram. Pribram taught that the brain has been, and likely always will be, mapped from diverse perspectives. There are circuits, networks, patterns, energy flows, functional areas, neurochemical paths, excitatory paths, layers, three-dimensional cycles, and more.

Pribram used the map metaphor to explain the multiplicity of forms of the brain. Specifically, a map that shows the current roads of an area looks entirely different from a map of mineral deposits or seasonal rain falls of that same area. In Pribram's work and the work of other neuroscientists, a map is not a simple artifice or metaphor. These scientists are on their own quest to understand the brain in its real shape, form, and pattern. This effort—to understand the most complex biological system on our planet—parallels our own personal work in the quest for presence: to witness this happening life in its fullest.

As you read below about the features of the map, keep this idea in the front of your mind: that a single pattern, form, or area can be mapped in different ways. Time, as we know, is an abstract topic to begin with. However, I believe it is easier to understand once we really grasp that time is, like the brain, one thing to view in different ways.

Perspective 2: A Graphic Rendering of the Map

In creating a graph to represent our metaphorical map, let's describe its basic elements. First, this map is continually woven out of time. It is not made up of elements in space, like parchment, tablet, or paper. Instead, it is made up of moments and occasions. These moving, shuttling threads are the most basic material of our map.

Moments. Imagine your life story, your treasure hunt, as an emerging tapestry. Each stitch of the needle of time is a moment. Like a star in a constellation, a moment contributes to a bigger picture. As you fully embrace your treasure hunt, your tapestry sends you a central and ongoing message: Special forces are always at work, pulling and pushing that needle through the fabric of your life, up and down, left and right.

Occasions. Our story is not only about our own threaded lines. Other threads journey with us, merge, veer, depart, and sometimes merge again. Occasions are those moments where we connect, when we are truly with others. Beyond the clock, time holds the many twists and turns of co-journeying. Wonderful occasions where we connect with what happens in the moments and when we are with others arise as time evaporates. We lift the surface veil of clock-time to see the beautiful complexity of life; it is much more than a solo journey. Likewise, our QfP is not only about self-help. It is best used with others.

A map with multiple levels. Imagine our map has many layers. The threads and weaves of moments and occasions are constantly moving across and within these layers. When we think about the journey of our life, we tend to use metaphors like *embarking on a journey, following a path, moving toward our destinations, reaching goals, taking sidelines.* But these metaphors refer to travels on the map's surface. They betray deeper dynamics. You are invited to find a more comprehensive perspective. Think of the map in three dimensions or having three vantage points: the surface, the layers beneath the surface, and the ongoing and incessant weaving of these layers as they connect with each other. For example, right now, in the moment as you read this, something is weaving through your life journey. This "something" can be known, whether it is obvious or mysterious; and it always involves wisdom, knowledge, intuition, or direct awareness of the very engaging and powerful process of being alive.

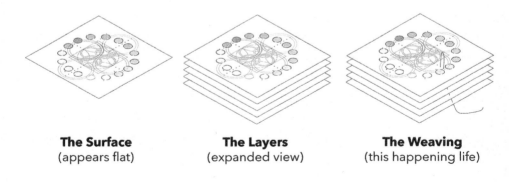

| **The Surface** | **The Layers** | **The Weaving** |
| (appears flat) | (expanded view) | (this happening life) |

Universal and Radiant Forces (The Directions)

Above, it was noted that forces are guiding the needle of time; your life is informed by four universal and Radiant Forces. The term *radiant* conveys that these forces are not single, straight lines. They are rippling energies or force fields that emit in multiple directions, constantly breathing in and out, expanding and collapsing like enormous spheres. These source energies are the basic building blocks of life that create your experience of time. Everything that happens is a result of how these forces unfold in your life. Briefly, these are the forces of Form (order, gravity), Chaos (entropy), Time Shaping (taking action, making things happen), and of things becoming (the Nurturing Conditions behind what is happening).

However, we rarely experience these forces directly. Our life is a frame for these forces. For example, we don't have an immediate and sensory experience of gravity; we have grown accustomed to it and take it for granted. And yet gravity, like the other three forces, is always there in the background. These forces live and work both outside and inside the frame that is our direct experience of this happening life.

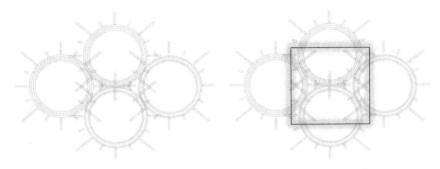

Radiant Forces

The Frame of
This Happening Life

Soulful Capacities

You can access and cultivate the four Soulful, or essential, Capacities in your journey. These are Acceptance, Presence, Flow, and Synchronicity (meaning embracing meaningful coincidences). These also may be called *time aptitudes* or *time competencies*. With these aptitudes, you can better see the true dynamics of the four forces, the multilevel map, and not get too caught up or stuck on the surface. To cultivate these capacities, QƒP offers in-depth exercises, self-assessments, and beginner's tools. The starter kit provided an initial self-rating. Later, in Books 2 and 3 and in the workbook, you receive a more comprehensive assessment of the Soulful Capacities.

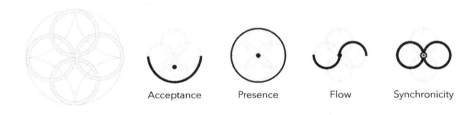

Acceptance   Presence   Flow   Synchronicity

Personality (Attractions)

Quest for Presence Inventory™ (or QFPI™) is a tool that helps you get your bearings within the (four) force fields in which you live. You will find the QFPI™ in Book 3. The QFPI™ helps you to see what *attracts* you among nine different tendencies (Attractions) within this field: Catalyzing, Intending, Coordinating, Centering, Discerning, Potentiating, Crafting, Opening, and Synthesizing. The Q*f*P starter kit provided an initial self-rating. The Q*f*P workbook provides the full self-assessment that is the QFPI™.

This part, or level, of the map is where most people think about self-knowledge, self-awareness, or knowing one's talents and short-comings. In our treasure hunt, the personality is intimately reflective of deeper attractions to Radiant Forces. I learned about this view of personality from various teachers in my life and was greatly informed by studying the spiritual Enneagram, or Holy Ideas as developed by Oscar Ichazo and the Arica School.

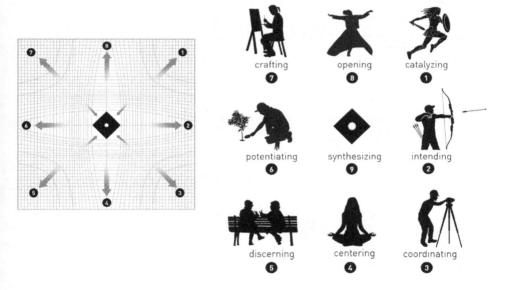

Let's pause and again name these first three aspects of our map: the Forces, Soulful Capacities, and Personality (Attractions). Elements within these areas interact with each other to either propel or pull you on your journey. Your personality is a reflection and is intricately woven from deeper forces and processes happening right now through the entire universe. At the same time, you have a soul, essence, or aspect of your being. Your essence is beyond your personality; it lives in an intimate relationship with more eternal forces. Personalities will come and go, as each of us is here on the earth for limited clock-time. Your soul or essence abides in a longer time beyond your knowing. Another guiding principle may help:

Your soul is here to work with and through your personality to help you through life challenges and help you see the Treasures of this life.

Daily Life (Trajectories)

Before exploring the Treasures, we first discuss the more regular or mundane aspects, situations, of daily living. Daily life is where we are, where we spend our time "on the surface." In a way, daily life is like a veil that keeps us from seeing the Radiant Forces and the Treasures. At the same time, this veil—daily life—is itself a weave of the deepest forces in the universe. The four Radiant Forces are always interacting with each other to bring about the different facets, or Trajectories, of our daily life. And you will learn about eight different Trajectories: Routine, Scheduling, Transition, Timing, Rhythm, Transcendence, Interruption, and Pacing. Everything that happens "in our day" is a function of these Trajectories.

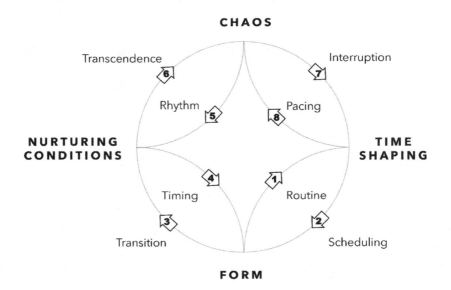

The Treasures

The Treasures make up another aspect of our multilayered weaving. These are available to us "in our day," in our lives, through our souls, and within our personalities. The Treasures are everywhere and really are about loving life. The sixteen different Treasures emerge *because* of your Soulful Capacities and how your soul dances with the four Radiant Forces. These Treasures are Spontaneity, Momentousness, Fulfillment, Clutch, Optimism, Effortlessness, Ordinariness, Coherence, Adoration/Charm, Harmony/Resonance, Patience, Preciousness, Savoring, Poignance/Forgiveness, Release, and Awe/Humility.

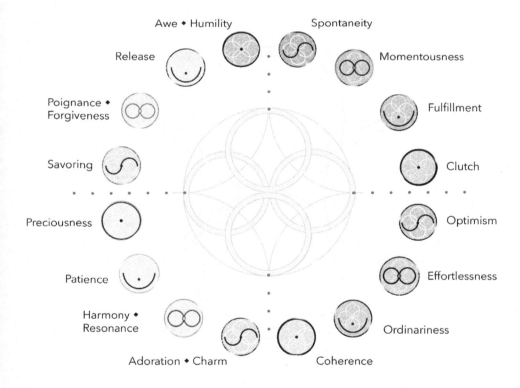

Putting It All Together

When viewed in this graphic manner, it certainly seems that our life is a complex makeup of many processes. Again, life is complex, but it need not be complicated. It is all about seeing the big picture. QfP will teach you to treat time in a way that allows you, day after day, to get a clearer view of that big picture.

I work really hard at trying to see the big picture and not getting stuck in ego. I believe we're all put on this planet for a purpose, and we all have a different purpose ... When you connect with that love and that compassion, that's when everything unfolds.

~ ELLEN DEGENERES (AMERICAN COMEDIAN)

The big picture doesn't just come from distance; it also comes from time.

~ SIMON SINEK (AUTHOR, INSPIRATIONAL SPEAKER)

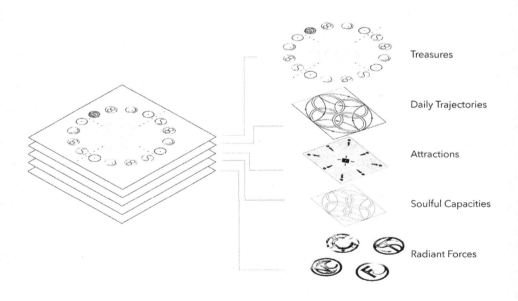

Treasures

Daily Trajectories

Attractions

Soulful Capacities

Radiant Forces

Contemplation (QfP 1-3):
See the Big Picture

Contemplation QfP 1-1 encouraged you to reflect on the big picture. This next contemplation asks you to actively see the big picture, the totality of the process of this happening life and your quest within and through it.

+ **From Perspective 1 (QfP Course of Study):** Which of the three objectives is most important to you? Which of the eleven ideas most interests you? Why?

+ **From Perspective 2 (Graphic Rendering of QfP):** How do you see your life as an unfolding weave or tapestry? Have you ever had moments, occasions, insights, or awakenings where you have glimpsed the bigger picture? What happened?

   Now, take some time to review the diagram or mandala at the very front of this book. This is the frontispiece on page iii.

Introducing the Treasures

Ode to Treasures

Youth is not some abstraction:
"A childhood filled with spontaneous impulse"

> Instead, consider that Light once sprung raw and
> from within you!
> Into and then right through the oven of life
> Exploding out the other side
> And right round again

Neither is aging:
"Some sweet reminiscence in the golden years"

> Instead, Light will just steal right through your brain
> like sparkles
> And then frolic all around you!
> You will know these particles were always there
> As your life is always here

~ J.B.

want you to first recall experiences, those where you had the sense of surprise, wonder, excitement, or a spontaneous surge of energy because you felt, "This is happening *now*!" For example:

✦ The sound of jingles coming from the *Mr. Softee or Good Humor* ice cream truck as it weaved its way through the neighborhood. You stopped everything you were doing and rushed to catch it.

+ That first time you caught the eye of someone—a desire, a pang, a sudden knowing, "This is the one"—and fell in love.

+ Standing on a stage and receiving applause, a diploma, or some other recognition, or delivering your first speech or performance.

In any of these, note how you were deeply immersed, embedded within, and even caught up in the event. There is no way to separate your full self from what was unfolding moment to moment.

Also, note memories of others within your happening life:

+ first learning you or your partner was pregnant;

+ the momentous kiss at the wedding;

+ being there as a loved one was dying: the moment of death, the funeral;

+ being there when someone was born;

+ meeting a teacher;

+ watching a movie;

+ reading a book;

+ listening to a song that changed your life.

Perhaps the moments are those shared across a nation or the world. I can access a distinct memory, a sensation in my gut, heart, and throat, from the moment when I first heard that John F. Kennedy had been assassinated on November 22, 1963, when the astronauts landed on the moon on July 16, 1969, or when I got tickets for ten of my friends, my math teacher, and his wife to go see Elton John in a solo concert at Carnegie Hall on June 11, 1971, and when those planes ripped into the Twin Towers on September 11, 2001.

In every one of these and many other life instances, I had a distinct sense that *this is happening now*. I accepted what was happening. I was present to it. I flowed with it. And, in many instances, I felt something momentous, mysterious, and sometimes even magical. Life was much bigger than I previously thought it could be.

Reflect

Consider that these more momentous events are not confined to some special time in our lives. Imagine that they are always available. You may think, "Really? Not *every* moment!" Yes. Every moment. There is a new emerging science of time, from studies of spiritual experience, from quantum physics, and from brain science, that suggests that this "life is happening" experience is available. Just because we may not be able or present to access or find it does not mean that it is not there.

So, imagine for a moment that the Treasures of this happening life are lying about underneath the surface of our day-to-day comings and goings. Several factors keep us from knowing this truth. Either, as I mentioned above, we think that the only type of time that exists is clock-time, or we have not been taught how to recognize or intentionally look for these Treasures. This is like not having a map or any tools on an archaeological expedition. Finally, and most importantly, we carry dark spots in our lives: unresolved conflict, previous trauma, current anxiety, depression, poverty, addiction, or some illness or disorder that sucks energy away from this happening life.

REFLECTION

Again, I have two memories, time traces, when I was about sixteen years old. In the first memory, I was on the second airplane trip in my life, from Kennedy Airport (Idlewild Airport back then) in New York City to Love Field in Dallas, Texas, for a family visit. My father, brother, and new stepmother were with me. I was seated near the rear of the plane, and the sky seemed so wide as I gazed out the window. In that moment, I was happy. The aircraft Muzak played a new and upbeat song, "Don't Cross the River," from the soft-rock band America (with lyrics by Dan Peek). At that very same moment, we were just crossing the Mississippi River. I felt exhilarated by the coincidence and meaning of the song. I was watching, for the first time, the wide, restless, and glistening river as we passed over. The changing pattern of glinting light captivated me. The uplift from this experience was a triumphant moment in my passage through an otherwise very rough, emerging adulthood.

The song tells the story of a young girl trapped in a lonely place. It requires crossing a river to leave, but there are no bridges to get out. The songwriter calls to her and says she can leave, forget her worries, and he invites her to ride on his own train instead of having to risk problems by swimming over by herself. He tells her she can "lose yourself and save some time" from further sadness, worry, and grief.

I needed to lose myself. My parents had divorced several years earlier, but only after I had endured a childhood riddled with their emotional estrangement, extramarital affairs, alcohol, depression, rage, and, consequently, my own anger, anxiety, and acting out. At the time of the trip to Dallas, I had been living with my despairing mother. I had tried to get out a few years earlier by crossing a bridge: the second memory.

After an intense argument with Mom, I had stormed out of our apartment in Far Rockaway (a town in Queens, New York) and just began walking to my father's apartment in Rego Park. I made it over the Cross Bay Bridge, past Howard Beach, almost to Ozone Park, more than ten miles away, before I called Dad. He didn't help. No one helped. I felt alone. I craved peace. I needed a break.

It is now 2020, fifty years later, and I stopped running away a long time ago. My mighty father's second marriage failed. My beautiful mother struggled with depression before she passed away a few years later. I still feel waves of grief. As I reflect back, that airplane song was a message, like a soundtrack to the movie of my adolescence. It took some time to figure it all out, but there really is no "other side" of the river that holds some promise or treasure. Instead, the treasure lies in losing oneself. Actually, it is in throwing oneself into the very effort to make it across, whether by walking over a bridge, by swimming the tide, or, most wonderfully, riding on that train with a friend or two.

None of us needs to struggle after things because we feel trapped. None of us needs to be alone. We can lose ourselves in being with what is happening now in our lives. We can feel connected. We can save ourselves from grieving.

There are always bridges out.

These bridges are treasured moments of beauty, freedom, absorption, and connection. Anyone can experience these moments, even on a regular basis. They may not always be "triumphant," but they will keep coming. I believe I have found a way, a richly terrained map, to help find them. I want you to experience these Treasures of life, to know they are there and how to find them. If you want, you can ride my train.

* * *

The story of my airplane song is one of dozens that I could have shared. All of us need to share these stories more frequently, especially in a world where people despair for the perceived lack of bridges. I share mine as a reminder you have a co-journeyer, and as an example of the unique ways the Treasures may reveal themselves in life. You will find additional stories of mine throughout Q*f*P. On this quest for presence, you are encouraged to understand and share your own stories (visit presencequest.life).

National surveys indicate that people spend increasing amounts of their time with technology rather than interacting with others. Our "connections" are often through a screen (computer or cell phone) rather than face-to-face. We also spend less time in nature and more time looking at photographic captures of nature. Look around. People are more folded into themselves than they are witnessing the unfolding of nature around them. You may personally not have this problem but may know others who do, and it may bother you.

Added to this, we have increased workloads, workaholism, and general clock-time compression. In short, we spend more time either working too much or mindlessly absorbed in media. We seem to prefer spending time with a mediated world streaming to us than with the true stream: the fully somatic, immediate, ever-changing, and natural sense-world. We are disengaged from the world that allows us to appreciate and immerse our very beings, our souls, in this wonderful, happening life.

We are captured more by the external packaging of light in modern-day media than by our own natural and internal light. The invention of the photograph, movies, the internet, and all new technology can be traced to discoveries about the nature of light and time. This began with Isaac Newton in the late 1600s and continued through scientists such as Michael Faraday and James Clerk Maxwell in the 1800s. Since then, the scientific application of light and time in the outer world of business and society far outpaces their application in the inner world of our souls. Commerce (time that is bought and sold) is more compelling than commerging (time that we flow with).

For many, the purpose of their own quest for presence is to change this formula, to empower themselves and others to view time in a new, healthy, and inspiring manner. It is time to renew our human, beauteous, and compelling sense of time; this is a sense that will outlast any technology. The saying, "Life is brief," is often followed by some call to manage your time as you move ahead: Find your purpose! Make the most of life! Get your priorities in order! Or even, Get a life, already!

But what if life's brevity is calling us somewhere else? Perhaps that is to a place that requires a more articulate, profound, and stunning vision of time. Maybe it's not all about just moving forward. Maybe life is about moving around, above, under, behind, over, as well as through time. New research on time in physics, quantum mechanics, and brain science suggests as much. Treasures are everywhere.

Treasure Stories

Later in QfP (as though this page is "now," and subsequent pages exist in the "future"), you will be encouraged to complete an exercise that asks you to recall and find different types of Treasures. Below are some "treasure stories" that I have been honored to gather from others. As you read them, please reflect on whether they stir something in you or remind you of a time in your own life. A hidden Treasure, or two or three, is revealed after each story.

Our home is in an urban part of a large county with rural areas. My husband and I took our young grandsons to the county fair to see the many animals brought from around the region. We came to a pen with llamas. One walked up to the fence, and I began stroking his face. He seemed to lean in. I began pressing my thumb onto the top of his nose. I gently pressed on the surface of his nose, between his eyes, and then onto the top of his head. He leaned in more. I repeated this caressing motion until we were chin-to-chin. Both our heads now raised to the sky. It was a moment of peace, harmony, and pure joy I will never forget. ⧗ *The Treasure of Connectedness in the Ordinary* ⧗

My father died on the night of my eighth birthday. Right afterward, my family sent me away from my home for a while. I missed the funeral. Throughout my childhood, my immediate family rarely even mentioned my father. But I knew. My grandmother and aunt lived upstairs, and they were heartbroken! Fast forward fifty years to my life today. Through personal self-work, I now cherish insights that bring meaning to this childhood trauma and in

my life every day. First, I clearly see how this family suppression was mentally unhealthy. I was literally taught to "de-press" my deepest thoughts and feelings. This insight helps me understand a lifelong struggle with depression. Second, I now have a label for my feelings, bringing self-compassion for my own inner child when I feel deep anxiety or sadness. Third, I have young grandchildren. Being around them sometimes triggers these childhood memories. But, instead of being overcome, I can be fully with them and positive because of my insight, self-care, and labeling skills. Overall, my life has more meaning, and I look forward to each day in a way I never have before. ⧖ *The Treasures of Coherence and Optimism* ⧖

∞

I was standing on the side of a four-lane expressway. The downpour was so cold. I remember thinking in amazement, "How is this rain and not snow spewing from the damn gray sky?" The very next moment, I felt the car touch my skin, I saw the headlights, and heard the blaring horn. I remember this as if it happened six seconds ago instead of six years ago. To say it was momentous would be quite an understatement.

I had been going through a divorce. Anger underlaid most of my decisions. I was driving my ex-husband's car that I had just received as part of our divorce agreement. So when I got a flat tire, I went straight into a seething blame mode. I called him. We were a LONG way from healthy boundaries at the time. I yelled "It is your f***ing fault … I am stuck out in the stupid rain with a stupid car with a broken stupid tire!" He begrudgingly told me to stay put. He would come change it. While waiting the thirty minutes for him to arrive, I had plenty of time to ramp up my attack. Apparently, he had a similar strategy. As soon as he got there, we both went straight into a "this is your fault" screaming match, on the side of the highway, in the rain. Freezing cold rain. I decided I didn't have to put up with the situation any further. I stormed to the car, flung open the back door, ripped my work bag out of the back seat, and in doing so stepped backward right into oncoming traffic. How the car didn't kill me, I don't know. Luck? God? Call it what you will. I physically felt, heard, and saw what could have been my death swerve through the rain to avoid striking me dead on.

It took me days to wrap my head around the immenseness of what could have happened. When it did, I felt a deep blessing and gratitude beyond anything I knew was possible. If you ever are lucky enough to experience getting hit by a car and walking away unscratched, you know in your soul what it means to appreciate every second as if it is your last. ⧗ The Treasures of Momentousness and Preciousness ⧗

∞

My life had become busy, complex, fragmented. I was not really living, just jumping from one activity to another. I longed for simplicity, for peace—to be present in my relationships. I practiced mindfulness for years, but it was not giving me peace. Things had to change. I decided to leave my twenty-year career. I began a "sabbatical" by taking a series of hiking trips to clear my mind and explore a refreshed sense of my life potential and openings. I prayed daily for a simpler life. I knew I was going to return to a new career, but I had no idea how this prayer would be answered.

My hikes were beautiful, day-to-day living, out of my backpack. When I returned, I simplified in every area of my life from what I ate and what I owned to commitments of time. I stopped multitasking. For each decision I made with my money and time, I asked: "Does this bring me peace, support my relationships, allow me to be present?"

The time to return to work approached. And it was just then that my stepchildren's mother unexpectedly died. With young, grieving teenagers, my life quickly became retirement from the workplace. As a full-time homemaker, I now share the routines of simplicity at home that I have been practicing for myself. Our *home is peaceful, our relationships are strong, and the children are thriving.*

Simplicity brings peace, and finding simplicity has been a journey—not of pilgrimages, mindfulness, and self-help books— but of trial and error and really slowing down ... everywhere (in space and time)! Slowing down has not always been easy or comfortable, but I can now savor each day, fulfilled in the simplicity of the routines of daily life. To me, that is priceless. ⧗ *The Treasures of Ordinariness, Release, Savoring, and Fulfillment* ⧗

∞

I was about twenty years old. That, of course, is the time in life when I knew everything. (It didn't last.) I was having an argument with my parents, and I was getting frustrated because I was losing, and I knew it. But rather than admit my defeat, I got up in a huff and shouted, "I'm done talking! I'm going to bed!"

So, I stormed down the hall to the bathroom to get ready for bed. Still seething, I arrived in my room to see that my father had left me a note.

On the note was a picture of Jesus at his Baptism with the caption, "You are my beloved son, in you I am well pleased." And he signed it, Love, Dad.

Almost fifty years later, remembering that night still brings tears to my eyes. Instead of condemning me for my misguided, self-important, twenty-something outburst, he reminded me of the best in who I was (and am). Instead of telling me why I was wrong and he was right, he just pointed out he could see something better in me.

I try to live up to those words still today. Although his physical body died in 2003, his love and his belief in me still live in what I do and how I try to live up to his words of encouragement. It has been more motivating to me than any other event in my life. Thanks, Dad. ⧗ *The Treasures of Momentousness, Adoration, and Poignance* ⧗

∞

Emotion, beauty, and goodness reside within each of these stories. They were written in response to a simple assignment. Throughout QƒP, you will be asked to simply reflect on moments of meaning in your life, of times when you are or were present. There is a significant chance that you have one, if not many, similar stories. Treasures can show up in obvious ways. Often, they are just glints, waiting to be noticed in the corners of our lives. They are the presents of our presence. They are the lasting, in some ways eternal, moments of quality that we value.

These Treasures don't just happen. They do not appear out of nowhere. While they are hard to predict, they also emerge as a function, a tango of time and your soul, across the dance floor of this lifetime. The Treasures arise from a meeting between the deepest aspects of your being and cosmic forces that transcend and shape your experience of time. Book 5 in QƒP contains practices you can do to increase the chances of finding a Treasure. Further, your unique personality—the Attractions—gives you access to different Treasures.

You also may notice something about time in the above stories. Sometimes, Treasures last just a moment. At other times, they sparkle through a longer situation, an accumulation, a transition, a teaching, a lifetime. That is the nature of the Treasures. They are there waiting.

There is a quotation by the poet and mystic Rumi that captures the nature of the Treasures: "What you are seeking is seeking you." The journey of life is not only toward something, some goal. Time is more like a beautiful, undulating ribbon than a straight, taut line. We simply have not been taught to see it that way.

Yes, that's right. Time is not only something to be managed. It is not a tool. Indeed, you will be encouraged to go far off the clock. Time is more of a friend, a companion, and a loving guide on the miraculous journey of your soul's life. And, as a journeyer, you and others in your life can, may, should, must, discover the various soulful and light-filled gems available every day. Why wait? Life is happening.

Contemplation (QfP 1-4):
Glimpse the Treasures

✦ Think about your earliest immersive experience of this life as happening now! What about being in a lonesome place? Of losing yourself? Of seeking a bridge out?

✦ Do you agree that time compression, workaholism, and commercialization of time are problematic? What are alternatives or positive perspectives?

✦ Which of the "treasure stories" most resonates with you? Why?

✦ What do you make of this sentence? "The Treasures arise from a meeting between the deepest aspects of your being and cosmic forces." Do you believe that one's experience of Treasures can be developed or cultivated?

The Treasures are interior and involve intra-sensory perception of deep feeling. Treasures have analogies or are captured by certain phenomena we see in the world. These manifest as things like gemstones, jewelry, flowers, stars, uncut crystals, seeds, snowflakes, and—for those with an inclination toward cosmology—galaxies, nebulae, and a whole range of astrophysical phenomena. Below is the same image from Contemplation QfP 1-1. I highlighted or bolded each treasure along with an image, randomly placed to convey how we may glimpse treasures among everything else that happens in life (the grayed text). They peek through. Compare this image with the one from Contemplation QfP 1-1. Notice how this image draws your attention in different ways. Which treasures happen to stand out for you?

release

 resonance

PRESENCE

 spontaneity   preciousness

Scheduling

 coherence   Interruption   Transcendence

TIME SHAPING   NURTURING CONDITIONS   forgiveness

 optimism

Routine   Rhythm

 momentousness   CHAOS   clutch

Timing

 harmony

FLOW   patience   ACCEPTANCE

 adoration   savoring

 awe   TRANSITION

FORM   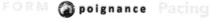 poignance   Pacing

SYNCHRONICITY

 charm    ordinariness   fulfillment

 effortlessness

CHAPTER 5

The Time Adjustment Protocol

Ode to Practice

So many practices to choose from
That might just lift you above it all
Or make it worthwhile
Or save you from yourself
Or just take your mind off things

Try one
Try them all
Maybe something will break in
And wreak holy havoc

~ J.B.

You were meant to be here. This is the next moment in the rest of your life. Your physical body may be time-limited, but your essence is timeless. Earlier, we described the frame part of the map. Again, these forces live and work both outside and inside the frame that is our direct experience of this happening life.

A Picture Frame Exercise

Imagine your life as a picture frame with four sides. The left and right sides are the beginning and end, respectively, of life: birth and death.

The bottom is time. The area—including and radiating from the center—is the present. The top is timelessness, and it has breaks or open spaces that allow your consciousness (energy, ideas, feelings, memories) to flow in and out of the frame. These four sides frame your life as it is happening right now.

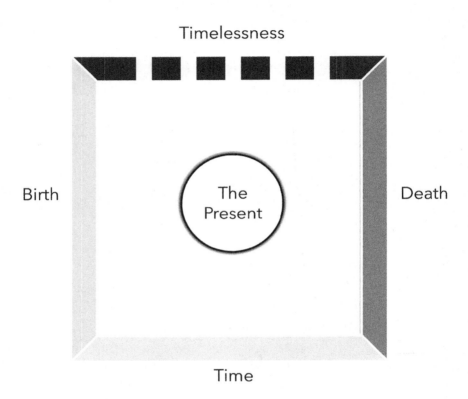

Visualize yourself sitting back, relaxing. Imagine the following four steps unfolding within this frame:

Step 1. Notice that you sometimes worry, get anxious, or get caught up in thoughts about the future or past instead of just being in the moment.

Step 2. Imagine that for just a moment, you stop worrying. Recognize that worry, anxiety, and obsessing are mental states that come and go. Let them go. They reflect natural processes. Everyone experiences worry to some degree at different intensities and different times. Realizing this, you refrain from judging yourself for how your mind works. It is just your mind's nature to do what it does.

Step 3. As you release these thoughts, you get more immersed in your life. Step inside the picture frame. Live your life instead of getting caught up in your mental chatter.

Step 4. Finally, you embrace the here and now (the center of the frame, the present). Life's Treasures unfold, and the entire picture takes on a *precious* and endearing quality. You are in the frame, and it also holds you gently.

You can repeat these steps a few more times. If you feel some relaxation, that is good. No need to worry about getting it right. Again, you are empowered to see time in a new and healthful way. This includes seeing challenges differently.

Mental Problems Are Reflections

Have you ever heard either of these sayings or something like them?

> *"Your soul will not place you in a situation you cannot handle."*

> *"Everything that happens in your life is for a purpose."*

Such sayings may be offered in comfort when we face a life challenge, tragedy, or injustice that is beyond our ability to comprehend. These sayings offer wisdom about being fully present to the situations, the happenings they refer to.

Many problems come from a lack of **Presence**, from having a poor relationship with time. Here are the main ways we avoid the present.

✦ We worry about the past and what we should or could have done.

✦ We think too much about the future and how we might manage it.

✦ We fret or stay anxious about what we cannot predict or control.

✦ We ruminate; that is, we get stuck in a loop of repeating things (often negative things) over and over in our minds.

Returning to our picture frame exercise, we can see that these four mental challenges keep us bouncing around the frame instead of being centered in the present moment. Indeed, most of us spend most of our time bouncing around, with our thoughts meandering in different directions ("mind wandering"). Brain scientists call this a "default mode," meaning that the general resting state of our brains is not directed to any particular activity, simply because we don't direct it.

As you consider this, recall Step 2 in the exercise above: Do not judge yourself for how your mind works; just see the state of mind for what it is as it comes and goes. The entire universe works in a similar way. That is, the mental processes of human beings are not only part and parcel of physical laws; they also reflect those laws in specific ways.

Our minds also tend to distort the natural way the universe works. All spiritual writings describe these distortions as vices or pitfalls and include fear, pride, addiction, anger, greed, envy, gluttony, and lust. Let's look at natural, real, and neutral factors in our minds that lie behind these distortions.

Four Mental Processes

Memory reflects to us that we are ever becoming. First, human memory is a real thing. As past conditions have led to our current situation, it makes sense we would turn our attention to them. Much of our life requires remembering and learning from past insights, lessons, teachers, and guides. In many spiritual traditions, it is considered a boon or gift to recognize how our past (no matter how painful) has truly facilitated our current and better circumstances.

Intention reflects the fact that we shape the future. Second, our intentions and the actions that stem from our intentions are also real. We are always moving into the future. We always have a hand in shaping the future, with chances to experiment, explore, work, imagine, and create new opportunities.

Attention reflects the fact that change, even sudden change, is inevitable. Third, our attention and our need to be vigilant are also real. Things are impermanent; the world is not always safe. It has many surprises, and life can be scary. Death is inevitable, and it can come at any time. So vigilance—being highly aware of our current state and our surroundings—is appropriate.

Labeling reflects the fact that nature has identifiable forms. Finally, our thinking and our use of words to identify or label our emotions and experiences are also real. Given impermanence and potential chaos and disruptions in life, it is truly functional that the mind would yearn for and find some stability in repetition, in turning things over, even if they are negative. Ideally, when we name things, we can tame them. For example, when we get distracted or have an "attention deficit," it helps to label what is going on. It helps to bring our wandering attention back from whatever disruption called it away.

These four mental processes—memory, intention, attention, and labeling—happen all the time; literally, all the time. To fully appreciate the role of these processes in our experience of "lived time," we only need to reflect on how they decline and degrade as our brain ages and approaches the final days of our life. The loss of memory to dementia and Alzheimer's disease is perhaps the most obvious. However, a significant body of research shows that all these mental processes fade. Simultaneously, the older we get, the less attention we pay to mechanical clock-time, the more we become immersed in the moment of nature, and the more likely we are to develop gratitude for being able to formulate and act on an intention at all.

In a way, as these mental functions fade, they start to give way to the universal forces that birth them. Each, in order, reflects the Radiant Forces described earlier. As the mental material of our happening life, they connect us with the universe.

1. Everything exists because conditions have radiated out from the past into the now and have helped them come into being. For example, the odds of you reading this are improved because of your previous education.

2. Everything is also subject to the law of cause and effect. Your past actions have radiated out and have led you to read this at just this particular point in your life. Likewise, reading this now will have some future consequence.

3. Everything is also subject to Chaos or decay. Everything will gradually dissipate, that is, radiate into nothingness. For example, these words that you are reading right now are fading impressions.

4. Despite these forces, all things also tend to have a recognizable shape or form: You have a body, identity, and other stable aspects of your life. The image of any form having radiance—the sun, a star, a work of art, a person—is something we can recognize. Things give off light, like this page.

Again, these are the forces: facilitating or Nurturing Conditions, our Intentions and behaviors and their consequences, Chaos and disruption, Form or stability. Each of these makes time show up in our lives. We can do a better job of listening to these forces; a well-lived life depends on listening to these forces. To listen well, we let go of distractions and clear our minds. Time itself is trying to teach you something. With the time you have left on this planet, you can discover your soul's capacity to handle your situation in this life. Indeed, the true situation is the whole time of your life.

Again, consider these two sayings: "Your soul will not place you in a situation you cannot handle," and "Everything that happens in your life is for a purpose." These ideas work together. When we know our purpose, we are more able to handle life situations. As we learn from loss, adversity, and grief, we demonstrate resilience and often get clearer about life.

We look back at our past and say, "Oh! I get it now. I had to go through that damn lesson so I can better address the obstacle before me now." This is not easy, especially when faced with trauma and significant loss. However, with a quality of intention, attention, and helpful labeling of experience, we can glean deep wisdom from our past.

We can adjust our whole experience of time, and we can experience time in its wholeness.

The Time Adjustment Protocol

Here are four basic suggestions that will help you on your presence quest. They comprise what I call a *Time Adjustment Protocol*.

1. You are already here; you might as well make the most of it (while it lasts).

2. Don't take any of it too seriously, except for a regular and dedicated practice that enhances your spirit, sense of meaning or purpose, or joy.

3. In every moment, you have the opportunity to see things as they really are.

4. Stay focused on taking positive steps toward your objective, and then sit back and enjoy the journey of your life.

This protocol is meant to empower you. You have power because you are already here. You may be caught up in the past or in some negative experiences that you feel have taken your power away. Use the protocol to find your power again.

Already Here, So Might as Well Make the Most of It

In the statement *Already here, so might as well make the most of it*, "here" can refer to this planet, your life's journey, and this particular moment. "It" refers to whatever time you have remaining. Tracing from the left side of the picture frame metaphor, certain threads have led you to now. Tracing to the right side, potential paths will lead from now into the future. You will next travel to one of several potential "worlds" of your future self. These worlds represent an amazing totality of possible scenarios that could occur in the frame. We don't really know where we will end up. To "make the most of it" requires a full, immersive experience and contemplation of life inside the frame.

Our minds—our imagination, intelligence, and creativity—provide a range of possible future experiences, hope, and optimism. Think for a moment about the immense totality or the fullness of all these possibilities. Part of you might feel lost, overwhelmed, or bewildered. Another part of you might feel some awe, humility, or inspiration. Actually, the greater your inspiration, the more you will milk life for all its potential.

Are you a child of your parents or a child of the universe? Are you a product of society, or are you the whole of all your own efforts at personal growth, aspiration, and education? Some people talk about a "bucket list," things they hope to experience before they "kick the bucket" or die. But what if every ordinary day was a bucket filled with feelings, insights, or contributions that were just as hope-giving and awe-inspiring as any special accomplishment? What if every day was filled with buckets just filling up, brimming with vitality, excitement, and joy?

To "make the most of it," consider your objective. This could be living simply and fully, enjoying happiness, success, or family well-being, following some cause or calling, or leaving a legacy. In my training work, participants sometimes share their objectives. When all else is stripped away, their "prime" objective often includes giving to others (often children), a heartfelt connection to some higher power, the universe, or a purpose that transcends their particular life. For most people, it is not about a series of buckets but about drawing from the immense ocean of life and filling only today's bucket to the brim.

REFLECTION

We always have the option of shortening our timeline. There were times in my earlier life when I wanted to kill myself, especially as a young adult. I was in such pain, or rather, in such void or emptiness, that I needed to call a therapist several times a day just to get through the next minute. Other times, my desire to hurt another was so great that I had to either run out of a house or stop and jump out of a car just to avoid doing something rash. These experiences sparked my desire to write this book. We can prevent suicide. Research indicates that suicidal thinking is linked to previous adversity (especially in childhood) and psychological states like pain, loneliness, depression, and impulsiveness. Significantly, adverse life events or trauma do not predict suicidal thinking. It is the combination of these risks with the lack of social support or the idea that support or compassion is forthcoming in time. Suicidal thinking and aggressiveness are also less likely when we have problem-solving skills, a sense of purpose, and the ability to reduce negative thinking. Family, friendship, and feeling connected (through time) are essential. These strengths are part of our Time Adjustment Protocol. Through them, we place ourselves in situations that continue into the future . . . the bridge to the other side.*

Don't Take Any of It Too Seriously

The mind will generate a plethora of challenges that block your view of the many possibilities of the future self that waits for you. By definition, any single mind (yours included) can see life only from a limited perspective. But there is always another way. So, it helps to have a sense of humor, a light-hearted appreciation, while you are making the most of it.

Life throws us curveballs. For example, things we thought we wanted at one time might turn out later to be bad for us. Or conversely, that which really helps us comes along out of nowhere and without much effort on our part. As they say, "Shit happens," "Every cloud has a silver lining," or "There but for the grace of God go I."

The only things we really have any control of are our behavior, our daily routine, our self-care. As American author and political activist Anne Lamott aptly writes, "Everyone is flailing through life without an owner's manual, with whatever modicum of grace and good humor we

---

* If you are concerned about suicidal risk, please seek help. In the U.S., please contact the 988 Suicide & Crisis Lifeline. Dial 988 or visit https://988lifeline.org/.

can manage." It matters greatly where we direct our attention. If any activity were to grace your attention, may it be one that enhances your spirit, your essence, or the deepmost vibrancy of your being, and may it keep you from flailing too much!

It would be a mistake to suggest that this type of spiritual or inspirational activity can come only from a religious endeavor. Such an activity often means a focused or intentional "spiritual" practice, one that enhances your sense of purpose in life. But please interpret this as liberally as possible; the activity or practice has to apply to you.

For readers wondering what I mean by spiritual practice, please refer to the boxed note on page 78.

Seeing Things as They Really Are

The "things" to be seen as they really are refers to all the content, the blur, whirling around the frame: sensations, thoughts, emotions, events, and so on. When not sleeping or dozing, we can be present to all of it, moment by moment. But the mind can be quite selective. It will show us only what we want to see. We are often zoned out, multitasking, or absorbed in a distraction like the latest technology. Still, the opportunity to see exists.

The phrase "as they really are" suggests an objective reality. Objective reality refers to the four Radiant Forces discussed earlier. It is a great irony of life. The very actions of our mind that keep us from being present at the same time reflect the deepest and most profound workings of nature.

Many spiritual practices, efforts to advance our growth, mirror these forces. They compel us to do four things:

1. Honor past methods instead of worrying about the past.

2. Do selfless service instead of just planning and managing our own self-centered lives.

3. Recognize impermanence instead of being anxious.

4. Repeat a spiritual phrase or affirmation instead of negative self-talk or preoccupations.

Let's pause to contemplate these hypothesized connections. The table below summarizes ideas across the mind, universal forces, and spiritual practice. For example, the unhelpful state of worry reflects the process of memory, which further reflects facilitating or Nurturing Conditions. The latter can be touched upon through the spiritual practice of honoring previous teachings. By doing so, we can reduce our worry.

CORRESPONDENCES AND REFLECTIONS: FROM UNHELPFUL MENTAL STATES TO SPIRITUAL PRACTICE			
These unhelpful Mental States (Shadow aspects of Treasures) ...	Reflect real "objective" Mental Processes ...	Which further reflect Universal Forces ...	Touched through Spiritual Practice
Worry about the past (Regret, Resentment)	Memory	Nurturing Conditions	Honor previous teachings
Overmanaging the future (Control, Manipulation)	Intentions and Actions	Action; Cause and Effect	Do good
Anxious about the unpredictable (Fear)	Attention	Chaos; Impermanence	Recognize impermanence
Rumination (Negative Self-talk, Judgment, Self-abuse)	Thinking	Stability; Form; Pattern	Practice focus through repetition

Note: Unhelpful mental states reflect real "objective" mental processes which reflect universal forces that can be touched through spiritual practice. For example, worry reflects memory which reflects Nurturing Conditions that can be touched by honoring previous teachings.

Seeing things as they are requires first recognizing, without reaction or judgment, the unhelpful mental states for what they are. Every religion or spiritual teacher warns us not only about worry but also about greed, jealousy, envy, fear, anger, and pride or attachment to our inflated view of ourselves. These "shadow" states are not how things really are. They are unnatural distortions of our true (or essential) self, our soul. Practices that enhance deepmost vibrance are designed to help us both embrace and diminish these shadow aspects.

Most spiritual traditions as well as modern psychology explain that we need to recognize two factors that give rise to these negative and limiting states. First, the mind likes to believe that we have a permanent individual self or ego. We fixate on, and reinforce through rumination, certain emotional states instead of seeing that these states are transitory. They come and go.

What Is a Spiritual Practice, Really?

Consider this quote from Saint Teresa of Ávila (Spanish mystic, 1515–1582): "We ought not to insist on everyone following in our footsteps, nor to take upon ourselves to give instructions in spirituality when, perhaps, we do not even know what it is." I interpret Saint Teresa's message to mean that each person needs to find his or her own definition of spirit, essence, innermost being, soul, or whatever term works for you. For example, each of the current major faiths of this world, such as Hinduism, Islam, Christianity, Judaism, Buddhism, holds its own definition of soul or spirit with many types of spiritual instruction. There are dozens of types of meditation practices. It would be nearsighted to promote only one type of spirituality as supreme or better than all the others.

In explaining spiritual practice, I wish to clarify three things. First, I do not advise a particular type of practice. Second, while the ideas in this book are not specifically offered as a spiritual practice, they may support your development whether you have a current practice or not. Finally, without *some dedication* to a *regular* practice, it may be difficult to appreciate some of the ideas about time discussed here. We all need an anchor, a centering tool, a set of coordinates to steady the flailing, keep us in the now on our journey.

In my experience, religions and spiritual practices contain the following features. They:

❖ honor some past teacher or guide who offered a method, way, or insights, sometimes through scripture.

❖ outline a path of taking action in a world that requires doing good, some level of devotion, charity, selflessness, and service to others.

❖ recognize that this temporal or time-limited world is impermanent, not the true reality. Even atheistic views uphold the latter idea. (Note. See Readings on Time Beyond Time (p. 138) and the QfP workbook for readings showing how this idea is represented across diverse traditions).

❖ teach a formal method of focusing the mind through repetition or a ritual.

You might notice that these four features roughly mirror the four processes introduced above: past conditions, taking action, impermanence, and form (see the table on page 77).

Different traditions emphasize some of these features more than the others. Most emphasize regular, daily repetition. Every teacher I have ever read or studied with says "Practice" or "Pray" or "Meditate," and do it every day. It can be a personal daily reading or devotional, sitting and watching the breath, repeating a spiritual affirmation or mantra, using prayer beads, or meeting with others to read and discuss scripture (such as the Bible, Torah, Bhagavad Gita, the Qur'an). It can be practicing a martial art, Tai Chi, Qigong, or yoga. It can be very personal and beyond any tradition: lighting a candle, going for a walk, meeting with a spiritual friend, being in nature, going to a particular spot in one's home or neighborhood to reflect and contemplate (sometimes, tea or coffee is involved).

Either way, the second part of the Time Adjustment Protocol indicates that finding one's "spiritual" practice needs to be taken seriously. You can laugh at all the rest.

Our personalities fuel this tendency. That's not to say there is anything wrong with personality; we all have one. Unfortunately, we tend to think our unique perspective is the only way, the right way, or better than that of others. Such thinking is the best way to take ourselves too seriously. We think that we are unlike others. We repeat our own stories about reality to the point where we believe them to be true. And we downplay the influence of others and the situation on our behavior. Consider:

> *I am always at a loss to know how much*
> *to believe of my own stories.*
> ~ WASHINGTON IRVING (AMERICAN WRITER)

> *When people are free to do as they please,*
> *they usually imitate each other.*
> ~ ERIC HOFFER (AMERICAN WRITER)

Seeing things as they really are requires being able to see ourselves over time: self-awareness, mindfulness of personality, understanding our cognitive biases and limitations. And it helps to see our self with a dose of humor. While self-awareness is quite difficult, considerable research suggests it is possible. We first have to see the lens through which we look at the world (our personality) before we can actually see how things really are.

The second factor behind limited thinking goes back to where we place our attention. Unhelpful states catch up with us; we focus on them instead of their opposite version (for example, anger versus serenity, resentful versus forgiving, feeling worthless instead of worthy). Indeed, every shadow has a light side: the Treasures. These states, where we glimpse the Treasures, reflect timeless qualities. In "The Treasures" section of the Q*f*P workbook, you'll find an exercise that invites you to recognize the shadow features of each Treasure.

Together, light and shadow represent the gifts of life and the operation of the four Radiant Forces.

Just as these forces are reflected in mental processes that can become rigid due to ego and personality, they also emerge in the positive, or Soulful Capacities. These capacities give us insight into how time really operates. They are much more fluid. They represent more essential and timeless aspects of our being. Tapping into these capacities requires using our attention in four different ways.

Soulful Capacities. The first, and most basic, Soulful Capacity is *Acceptance*. Peter McWilliams (an American self-help author) writes, "Acceptance is such an important commodity; some have called it 'the first law of personal growth.'" Acceptance is a function of past, facilitative conditions. We cannot change our past, so we learn to accept. The second capacity is *Presence,* or fully showing up. Thich Nhat Hanh, Vietnamese Buddhist monk, writes, "Without doing anything, things can sometimes go more smoothly just because of our peaceful presence. In a small boat when a storm comes, if one person remains solid and calm, others will not panic, and the boat is more likely to stay afloat." When we are present, we are both living in the moment and honoring the ongoing unfoldment of past to current conditions.

Flow is the most studied Soulful Capacity because of the late psychologist Mihaly Csikszentmihalyi's work. As a mental state, Flow occurs when we are fully immersed in performing an activity with energized focus and enjoyment of the process, not the outcome, of the activity. When we are in Flow, we are integrating our immediate previous conditions with the form or method we use in our action. Csikszentmihalyi writes, "Creating meaning involves bringing order to the contents of the mind by integrating one's actions into a unified flow experience."

Synchronicity integrates all the forces and the other capacities. Synchronicity is somewhat synonymous with grace.

The more we live in the state of happiness, the more we experience the spontaneous fulfillment of desire in the form of synchronicity and meaningful coincidence … To experience grace is to find ourselves in the right place at the right time, to have the support of the laws of nature, or "good luck."

DEEPAK CHOPRA (INDIAN-AMERICAN AUTHOR)

It is not only possible to cultivate each of these capacities, but it can be our purpose in life, our objective, to do so. We are truly fulfilled when we find Acceptance, achieve Presence with what is, learn to Flow, and find Synchronicity. When we do, we see things as they really are.

REFLECTION

It often takes courage to see things as they really are. Have you had a moment in your life when you suddenly knew that something was not right, that the situation you were in was either unhelpful, dysfunctional, or even dangerous? When I was about eleven or twelve years old, my father got angry at my brother and me for something. I don't remember the details. I do remember my father, a big man with the demeanor of a heavyweight boxer, picking me up in his arms and throwing me. At that moment, I could no longer deny the situation I was in. I had this keen sense of awakening, of seeing things as they really were. My parents divorced not long after that incident. I have learned to accept and forgive. Mostly, I've learned how to notice the negative self-talk and soften my feelings toward myself with self-compassion. Many years later, by practicing this Time Adjustment Protocol, I was able to forgive my father. And in his last years, he showed the Acceptance, love, and acknowledgment of me as well.

Sit Back and Enjoy the Journey

I am not advising you on your particular life objective. You must find that for yourself. Here is another quote that I have found helpful, from British philosopher Alan Watts: "The meaning of life is just to be alive. It is so plain and so obvious and so simple. And yet, everybody rushes around in a great panic as if it were necessary to achieve something beyond themselves."

Whatever your objective, I recommend the following: You view life as a journey; along the many paths that comprise that journey, take time for a spiritual path; and do your best to keep things as simple as possible. Take positive steps each day. Then, sit back and enjoy what happens. This may sound easier than you believe is possible. You may be faced with hardship, tragedy, trauma, illness, disability, or any number of challenges that just sap your energy and leave you sad. If these are your circumstances, I strongly encourage you to reach out for support and help; professional help may be needed.

To "sit back and enjoy the journey of our life" means many Treasures line the path. We can have moment-to-moment experiences of these Treasures. We only need immerse ourselves into this life without preconceptions, analysis, clinging, or getting too stuck in the mind and our distorted perceptions of time. In summary, life is short—enjoy the ride!

Contemplation (QƒP 1-5): The Frame

Try this activity. You will need a single piece of paper.

1. Draw a horizontal line across the longest side of the paper. Imagine this line to be the timeline of your life.

2. Write your date of birth at the very left starting point.

3. Then estimate, based on your current age, your life expectancy; for example, this could range between 50 to 100 depending on your lifestyle habits and where you live in the world.

4. Notice how far you have come to the present day. Identify whether you are before or after the midpoint on the line. Notice how much estimated time you have left.

5. This next step of the exercise is most important. Recognize that, for now, the line is but one single line. It is a thread among many possible threads you will explore in this precious weave of life. Thinking about how much "time" you have left, contemplate these questions:

  ✦ What are some of your possible objectives? Where does life add value?

  • What do I expect *to happen* before my time is up?

  • What is my intention? Where will I direct my attention?

  • What memories will I have? What stories will I tell?

  ✦ What steps, if any, are you taking in the direction of any of those threads?

  ✦ How does it feel to follow that thread? Now draw another line and think about where that thread may lead. Now draw another.

These are only example questions. Many things happen beyond what we may think our objective is. It is a mistake to think that life is only about achieving a goal. Most spiritual paths point to self-realization, of letting go of our limited self-views or ego, and then merging into some sense of love, service, unity, divinity, or relationship with the universe, spiritual forces, God, other deities, or a Higher Power. These objectives do not come at the end of our projected timeline. They are always, every day, available now. They are within the line (or any line) you just drew.

PART TWO

Four Radiant Forces

Ode to Time: Woven

The map worn, you set it aside
Revealing gems, hidden inside;
Ribboned lines enfold
The card once dealt you dearly hold.

The distant treasure was craved,
You gleaned the ocean in a moment's wave;
Your wandered self, wove in time
A precious thread in the Design.

Leave memory, leave sense; to reveal
Treasures on Now's smiling field;
Radiant forces beckon your soul:
With every step, this yarn turns gold.

~ J.B.

I am a fan of science fiction that involves time travel. The strict sequence of an unfolding life goes completely out the window. I am held captive by the emotions, meanings, and connections as the characters take center stage while time splinters, disintegrates, reappears, and moves around. Life becomes important. Time becomes playful. Sequence gives way to something more powerful than time itself. Time becomes more magical and uplifting. In the end, the characters and I come away wiser.

The purpose of the following chapters is to encourage you to look for the magic. Some readers may consider the idea of the Radiant Forces too abstract, ephemeral, or theoretical to have any real-life application. I invite you to explore this next section (part two) as creatively or impulsively as you possibly can. Read the next chapters in order. Alternately, hop around in a way that suits you best. Perhaps just complete the contemplation exercises at the end of chapters 6 through 10. Or, simply read my personal reflections, review quotes, or study the table in chapter 9.

The next chapters repeat (or view from different angles) hefty ideas that I believe lie behind the magic of this happening life. First, the forces represent the *Totality of Reality* and our experience of reality (see chapter 6). This idea is exemplified by Native American cultures and other native wisdom traditions that hold the idea that everything is alive on the earth and in the universe. When we hurt any part of the earth or the universe, we hurt the whole of the universe. The four directions in Native American culture are called the "sacred hoop" or "medicine wheel." No part stands alone and is defined by its relationship to the other. We see the big picture. Similar ideas are expressed in scientific theories about the holographic universe. Every part of our reality is represented from the smallest particle to the largest galaxy.

That everything is holding together or being held together represents the second idea conveyed about the forces (chapter 7). The forces depend on each other. Each one holds the other in its respective place. Each force creates the space for the others to manifest. Everything is held, and we are all part of the holding. This idea is seen in age-old practices about the role of spiritual community in India (sang-hat), the Christian church, the sacred tribe, and, most obviously, the family. The existence of families across many species (including trees and plants) speaks to this universal principle of holding together.

When we experience stress and anxiety that make us feel that "we cannot hold it together," it is because we are out of touch with the deepest reality that everything is being held together. We are all part of a family at some level. Chapter 7 describes ideas from the philosophy of Taoism that further illustrate this idea.

Forces are also always unfolding and are part of what make every-thing unfold. Chapter 8 begins to describe how the forces unfold to bring about the manifest reality that we experience as the sequence of time. As we are held in the totality of our own experience, or once we deeply know that we are being held, then everything starts to unfold. The forces act like a container into and through which the water of this life unfolds and happens to us. We are, all of us, sitting on the lip of that container watching as life, the Tao, unfolds.

The next idea is about listening for the forces in our lives and the resulting wisdom that comes from such listening. Chapter 9 gives four examples to illustrate how this works: when we fall in love, in sailing, gardening, and pottery. Wisdom comes from seeing how the forces work together in all of these examples so that we treat with respect and honor our life and the lives of others. Each of us may or may not glimpse the totality (chapter 6) or feel held (chapter 7) or witness the unfolding (chapter 8). Alternately, others may see the patterns described in chapter 9, and, in so doing, come to the realization of the totality, holding, and unfolding.

Chapter 10 is about discernment or the ability to most clearly see the operation of the forces most specifically. A more complete descrip-tion of each force is given, and you are asked to see how you can dis-cern the operation of the force in the moment.

CHAPTER 6

Totality

Ode to All

All is All:

The night sky,
Myths and legends,
Our ancestors and atomic orbitals.

We are all here.

~ J.B.

This chapter gives detail on our map because: 1) I want you to have more references to help you better identify aspects of the map; 2) it takes time and repetition to see the big picture; 3) the map is a companion tool to the Time Adjustment Protocol, use either one or both together; and 4) it helps to see the map as just another moment in time.

I have met different seekers who get tied to a particular school of thought, way of thinking, model, or guru. This attachment can limit their sojourn. Again, a map is only a tool and not the real, messy, living, and dynamic terrain of the process of your life. But it helps to have one in your back pocket for those moments when you need it.

The five features of the map make up our total experience of this happening life. Your life is whole and one, not a mixture of separate parts. It is one unfolding pattern that you will, from time to time, glimpse in its meaning. Remember that the precious qualities, the Treasures of Fulfillment, Contentment, and Release, for example, are not the real goal. They are part of the entire journey: a process of learning and discovery. The Treasures arise *within* and *through* the journey, not at the end of the journey.

The Precious Weave (The Totality of the Map)

Everything—and I mean everything*—is just a consequence of many infinitely large fields vibrating. The entire universe is made of fields playing a vast, subatomic symphony.*

~ DON LINCOLN (AMERICAN PHYSICIST)

Many astronauts, upon seeing the whole earth against the sky for the first time, experience what has been called the "big picture" or "overview" effect. Three core emotional features make up their experience: a sense of preciousness, fragility, and awe; a desire to protect the earth (including protecting it from political fragmentation); and a profound awareness of unity, wholeness, or interconnectedness. I want you to be able to look at your whole life in the same way.

It may help to locate and look at a map. Stand back and look at the big picture. A crisscrossing emerges, made up of many roads and paths, along with other traversing elements (railroad tracks, rivers, creeks). Some lines are straight, particularly manufactured ones, the "main roads." Most lines meander and travel only a short way. In the context of our journey, these lines represent a precious weave of the different trajectories, the stories, circumstances, and continual unfoldings, of our life on this planet. These lines contain the many emotions and feelings we have about these trajectories. In other words, this happening life is a precious weave. Our emotions help us directly experience the unfolding as it is happening.

Have you ever looked up at the night sky of stars, especially away from the lights of the city? This experience, just of our galaxy itself, can produce feelings of awe, humility, or inspiration. But there is more. Between September 2003 and January 2014, the Hubble Space Telescope photographed beyond our galaxy and much deeper into the universe than any telescope ever had before. These photographs reveal not only the most distant galaxies but also look back in time toward when the universe was in its infancy. These images clearly show how the universe extends in all directions throughout time (eternity) and space (limitless). Unfathomable. It is hard to believe that we are part of this eternal and limitless totality.

It is difficult to step back and see the big picture. Viewing the earth from space, we see one, whole, unified globe, when what actually exists is a blur of activity. The closer we get, the more natural formations and lines come into view. Even closer, we see manufactured features of lights, cities, buildings, roads, and so on. Regardless of how close or far we get, it is still one integral whole. There is a totality at all levels: the overview or big-picture effect. Unfortunately, we tend to live our lives, spend our "time," only at one level.

There are many reasons why it is difficult to step back and see the totality or big picture. We are extremely limited in what we can actually observe with our senses. But even these biological limitations are outweighed by self-imposed and cultural limitations. Again, consider our busy adherence to clock-time and eventual exhaustion, getting caught up in our day-to-day routines, taking life for granted, and focusing on negative emotional states, especially anxiety and irritation.

This is why it helps to have reminders of our original unity: spending quiet time in nature, meditation, spiritual readings, or finding mentors, teachers, or older people in our lives and communities— grandparents, tribal elders, senior citizens—who can weave big stories about the past. The myths and legends that help shape the story of a society help us to see the precious weave of our own lives: where we came from, where we are, and where we might journey to. All art and entertainment (music, poetry, dance, theater, movies) can help us to see and directly experience the precious weave. Further, new insights from science and cosmology suggest that the universe is itself a matrix of energy, much like a weave of information.

The precious weave refers to the ongoing nature of time as one, whole, and unified reverberation. This ongoingness is due to the four Radiant Forces that create, frame, and continually shape our tapestry.

Universal and Radiant Forces (The Directions)

Life is a process, life is a story, and we both shape and are shaped by this process and this story. Powerful forces govern our time. These forces influence not only our experience of life but also much, if not everything, in the universe. Our map is not two-dimensional or static. It is not in a fixed space, like on a sheet of paper.

It is a moving and multilayered array of flags, a carpet or rug, with threads of information gliding in different directions, continually buffeted by different winds or forces that blow in different directions. Time unfolds through these different forces, forces that beckon us, move us, and compel us to explore different sections of the map, to fully live our life.

Several images or analogies can help us better grasp the idea of these forces.

You, Your Life, is the Intersection of Forces. Imagine you are sitting alone in a room and hear a single note or tone of music. Now, analyze this sound further. You discover that you hear it all as one sound, when in fact, it is a convergence of different vibrations. These vibrations come from different tuning forks, each placed at equal distances from you.

Your experience lies at the intersection of these sounds, so you hear it as one sound. You may have had this experience listening at the center of a quadrophonic sound system, with four speakers surrounding you. Reflecting on the totality of the precious weave, imagine that this one note represents the universe. We experience *this one life*, but it consists of different vibrations converging onto a single space and time.

You, Your Life, is Ever the Center of a Map. Another analogy is the four directions on a map: north, south, east, and west. These forces correspond to phenomena we know from science. Briefly, there is the force that makes things come together, gives them shape, structure, form, and coherence. This corresponds to the force of gravity. Imagine this toward the south. In contrast, there is a force that makes things fall apart, to become random and chaotic. This corresponds to the force known in science as entropy (meaning the tendency for matter to move toward randomness). Imagine this toward the north.

There is also the force behind our own actions, of our observing, behaving, and having an influence on others and situations, as well as others and situations having an influence on us. This corresponds to the law of cause and effect in the physical sciences (for every action, there is a reaction) and the law of karma in Eastern philosophy. Imagine this toward the west.

Finally, a force exists within the deep pattern or abiding conditions of all natural and living systems. We would not be here without pre-existing conditions that support, energize, and sustain us on our journey. These facilitative conditions energize us to find nurturance, grow, emerge, self-organize, explore, and survive. And they also eventually lead to systems that subside, disintegrate, and decompose.

This force is the most difficult to understand. It corresponds to several concepts. This includes "self-organizing" systems in the biological and social sciences. Everything has a tendency to organize itself into a pattern. Even when life seems chaotic or you experience anguish and worry because of change, some pattern is emerging. This concept also exists in Chinese society and Buddhist thought as the doctrine of dependent origination. Everything we experience is dependent upon our senses and is due to a predestined, mutual connection or coregulating process that occurs between entities. Imagine this force toward the east.

You, Your Life, Always Has Direction. When we get lost without a map, a compass helps us get our bearings through the four directions. In Book 3 of QfP, you will learn a lot more about "getting your bearings," or coordinates, with a self-assessment tool. For now, using this metaphor of the four cardinal directions, think of the placement of the four Radiant Forces on our imaginary map as somewhat arbitrary.

Except, keep the idea that the directions stand in opposition, for example, toward the north versus south, toward east versus west. The idea that the forces oppose each other is related to the idea of opposition in yoga. When practicing yoga postures, one finds balance in opposition. For example, when balancing on one leg (as in a tree posture), you press the standing foot squarely into the floor as you lift erect your head toward the sky. When you lift up without pressing down, it is very easy to lose balance and fall over.

I also use the word "toward" a direction; wherever you are on the map, you always have the ability to move toward one or more directions. You are always "within" the directions. And, as we shall see, each of us is also uniquely "attracted to" different directions. Your ability to move around depends partly on your Presence to this happening life and on taking an attitude best expressed by the sayings, "No matter where you go, there you are" and "I don't know where I am going, but I am on my way."

You, Your Life, is Always Self-Correcting (Homeostasis). The forces work together in a give-and-take, reciprocal, or homeostatic way. For example, imagine we get lost in a forest. We get our bearings by returning to the path recently traveled. We go back. Much of this happening life is about returning.

If we came from the north, we head back toward the north trail; if we came from the east, we move toward the east trail. In a similar way, when our life gets stuck in routines (the work of gravity), we may tend *toward* the random and seek out novelty and fresh experiences. If we get too busy working and are always focused on achievement (the work of cause and effect), we can tend *toward* taking time for self-care and nurturing (the work of self-organizing systems). Our ability to self-correct is a sign of well-being.

You, Your Life, is a Unique Expression of the Forces. These tendencies toward directions (forces) are influenced by many factors, especially our personalities and our culture. In Book 3, you will be invited to complete a personality assessment (The Quest for Presence Inventory™) to help assess your tendency. You will learn how different careers, vocations, or hobbies use certain talents; for example, those with a tendency toward the northwest (nurturance and Chaos) may be most fulfilled in the creative arts; while those with a tendency toward the southwest (form and action) may be most expressive in the engineering or manufacturing fields.

Contemplation (QfP 1-6): Glimpse the Forces

STEP 1. First, reflect on the four paragraphs below.

1. The passage of time means there will always be mystery, new frontiers, and the unexpected. There is always the opportunity for novelty and discovery. It is all a matter of being open and abandoning preconceptions. Life innovates, has a wildness, a Chaos to it. Consider this quote:

> *Discovery consists in seeing what everybody else has*
> *seen and thinking what nobody else has thought.*
>
> ~ ALBERT SZENT-GYÖRGYI
> (HUNGARIAN BIOCHEMIST, NOBEL LAUREATE)

2. The passage of time means we have a responsibility to organize our lives to make the most of our time here. To pursue what attracts us. We should do our best to master time through setting priorities, establishing goals, and using tools to manage our time (such as using planners, calendars, schedules). A fulfilled life requires knowing our place in it. Consider this quote:

> *A place for everything and everything in its place.*
>
> ~ BENJAMIN FRANKLIN

3. The passage of time means everything brings forth moments for becoming and for us to understand, relish, and use for our own or other's growth. It is all a matter of paying attention to trends, cycles, timing, intuition. There is an art to knowing when the time is right for things. We get more out of life when we attune to it. Consider this quote:

> *To everything there is a season, and a time*
> *to every purpose under the heaven.*
>
> ~ KING SOLOMON, ECCLESIASTES 3:1 (KJV)

4. The passage of time means life requires action, (achieving results,) and accomplishing things. Life provides each of us a calling, a cause, a destiny, or a legacy to discover. We may not always leave a mark yet, we can at least make a good effort. It's all a matter of paying attention to, and taking hold of, the opportunities given to us. Consider this quote:

Carpe diem.

~ LATIN: "SEIZE THE DAY"

STEP 2. Second, which of the four paragraphs above do you feel the most drawn to, or have a life philosophy that fits the ideas expressed, or which most resonates with you?

Rank the paragraphs from the most preferred (#1) to the least preferred (#4).

The passage of time means:

	There will always be mystery ...	We have a responsibility to organize ...	Everything brings forth moments for living fully ...	Life requires action, achieving results ...
Most preferred (1)	☒	☐	☐	☐
Second preferred (2)	☐	☐	☐	☒
Third preferred (3)	☐	☒	☐	☐
Fourth preferred (4)	☐	☐	☒	☐

Take a look back at your response to the first exercise in your Q*f*P starter kit in chapter 1. How does your rank order fit with your earlier responses? As you continue to read, you will discover more about these four perspectives and how they reflect four different forces that "hold everything together" and that call you to journey.

CHAPTER 7

Holding

Ode to Holding

In the end, would you rather
hold or be held?

"Does it depend on what I am holding?"
   you ask;
I say nothing but repeat:

All is All
Holding All.

~ J.B.

Let's pause for a second. These ideas about totality, the big picture, and the four Radiant Forces are abstract. My understanding of them has saved my life. Literally. Previously, I described my own depression and suicidal thinking.

I am still just holding it together. But I understand "holding it together" in a different way now. I need to write this down, to tell you, or I might fall apart. Let's get it out in the open: I am going to die, and you are too. Our time is limited. Let's not be strangers.

For most of my life, when people asked me where I came from, I told them, "The beach." I was raised by my parents near the ocean, in an apartment about a half-mile walk to the beach in Far Rockaway, New York. But even as a child, in my inner being, I knew that "I," my keenest sense of being alive, came from some other place. This place was unorganized, deep, and primal. No location on any map. No origin. No position. No time. My dear departed friend, Dorinda Hartson, called it "The Elsewhere."

> *I did not descend from Adam and Eve or*
> *any origin story. My place is placeless,*
> *a trace of the traceless.*
>
> ~ MAWLANA JALALUDDIN MUHAMMAD RUMI

I thought I came from where the ocean meets the shore, where primordial life begins. The cells in my body were magically held together by some force, endowing them with the ability to find each other, coordinate, and somehow make this mind-body contraption work. These are some of the deeper questions that motivate my quest for presence: Where did we come from? Where are we headed? How can we really locate ourselves in the vastness of time? How are we holding it all together?

I have always been just holding it together. I have always felt that "I" will fall apart, disappear. In common human language: die. At any time, I can stop and scratch beneath the surface of my daily routine and feel time passing, slipping away, falling into nothing. Then, there arises a series of sensations and thoughts. Their essence: Life is and always has been utterly precious.

The feelings can seize, overwhelm; I stop. I feel my skin, my breath, my heart. Tears start. It is not grief. It is bigger than that and much closer to love than to sorrow. Then, to ground myself, I look out my window. I see people coming and going. I can't imagine how they manage. Don't they feel this, too?

Through all these reflections—our origins, my father, my mother, death—time is the underlying thread that I return to. The filaments inching along.

REFLECTION

During the time I was writing this book, my siblings and I buried some of the ashes of my father. He passed away on November 22, 2017, at the age of eighty-seven. At that time, we held a veteran's memorial service and funeral. I gave out his favorite Baby Ruth chocolate bars during the funeral as a wink to my dad's spirit. I decided to wait for the earth burial until the summer and did so just after the summer solstice. Hours after the burial ceremony, I returned alone to the cemetery in the latest part of the afternoon. I sat on the ground against the maple tree just a few feet from his grave. Upon reflection, I realize I always return alone to the gravesite after everyone leaves: for my mother, my grandmother, my mother-in-law, my father-in-law. I sit and listen, just as I did with my father, at dusk, in the farthest corner of that beautiful green sloping cemetery. After about ten minutes, the words from a song popularized by Don McLean, "And I Love You So," came to me. In the song, the "brief book of life" is a metaphor: after each page turns, nothing remains but love.

We all came from someplace long before "the beach." Different myths and religions describe how life came into being out of darkness, out of the expansion or contraction of the universe, or from some singular origin point. We only need to look up at the night sky to realize the vastness of this single space-time galaxy. The inescapable sense of vastness, of eternity ... so ineffable, and so lonely, dark, and terrifying. We will die. We will become nothing. We think.

This forms the constant face of our cosmic insignificance. Philosophers peer into it. They argue that we unceasingly create distractions to harbor, to *hold*, a sense of security. Through these human-made distractions, the moorings of civilization—education, family, marriage, occupation, or career—we define the only reality we know, along with our roles, laws, rules, social norms, arts, rituals, science, and politics.

We are holding it (our reality) all together. We overidentify with these things and seek to be right, grab for space, for dominion. We struggle to make a mark, make ends meet, make a career, and help our children make it as well. We try to fit in, be known, become something, or at least fulfill our roles. Success. Fame. Honor. Power. We are always in a hurry to do so before our time runs out. But all of this will, eventually, fall apart: "Once a page is read, all but love is dead."

REFLECTION

Like my father, I, too, often get impatient. Instead of "holding it together," I either "lose it" (become angry, irritated, frustrated) or get "caught up" (meaning ruminate, close off, obsess) within myself and my expectations. Many situations could be a trigger: the long line at the grocery store, my coworkers failing to get their projects done on time, the uncertain future of my business, my wife coming home too late for dinner. I wonder, "When will I ever get recognized for my accomplishments?"—and so on and so on. But something simple and profound happens when I sit down to reflect, to write, to meditate, to be near my father's ashes. Like right now. I am connecting to a deeper process. It is not only "this too shall pass," but also that all of us are here passing through this world ... together.

Other philosophers offer an alternative; dance with your cosmic insignificance, laugh at it. They point to the wisdom of insecurity, the illusion of time, the remarkable evolution of consciousness in humanity, our collective intelligence, our capacity for love that transcends time, and our time-worn capacity to foster and uphold truth, beauty, and goodness.

For example, in the philosophy of Taoism, the *Tao* (also spelled *Dao* and pronounced "dow") is translated as the way or the path. At the deepest level, Tao means the way to returning to one's original and essential nature.

In Taoism, everything is always the Origin: The universe has no beginning and no end. Let's use the gift of life to cultivate love, moderation, and humility. Let's learn to embrace and flow with the moment. From this perspective, time does not weigh us down or march along. Instead, it is our ever-present friend and teacher, always there, always sustaining us. If things arise or come into being, it is the way of the Tao. If things unite together, it is the way of the Tao. If things fall apart, disintegrate, or die, it is the way of the Tao. And, throughout it all, the Tao sustains all things.

To witness this happening life, we must release the illusionary pressure of time, one that eats away at our health and our soul. It is a false pressure. We have succumbed to an artificial, mechanical, manmade clock-time. We have been led to believe clock-time has a positive purpose: to help us plan, to conform to routines of daily life, of commerce, and to negotiate our way through life. Too often, clock-time lures us into a prison. It cajoles us into buying and selling, pushing buttons, and mindlessly giving away information that belongs to our sacred, private self. Most important, and the purpose of this book, is that this runaway and blind acceptance of clock-time has led to us spending less time with each other: directly, face-to-face, intimately.

So now, I still believe that I came from the beach. I also came from no single place and everywhere. I don't know where I am going, but I am on "the way." I can buy into the fabrication of clock-time when I need to, and when I am conscious and I pause, I can tune into another sense of time: real time, with you. What if, at some deepest and most true level, we are all being held together?

Contemplation (Q*f*P 1-7):
Holding It Together

Where did you come from?

How did you get here?

What have you lost?

Who have you buried?

How are you holding it together?

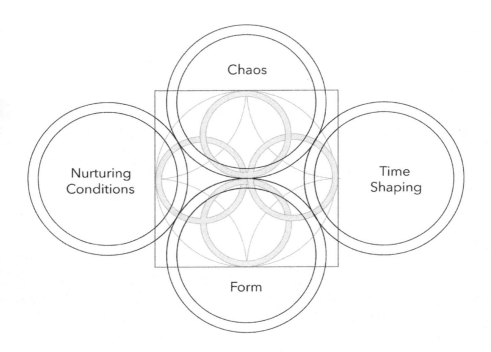

Form	**Chaos**	**Time Shaping**	**Nurturing Conditions**
Gravity ● Structure	Entropy ● Dissolution	Causality ● Action	Context ● Becoming
A Call to Order	A Call to Create	A Call to Act	A Call to Wait & Align

CHAPTER 8

Unfolding

Ode to Unfolding

What can a vacuum do with an
    empty space?
Or a void do to an empty vessel?

Black holes dress it up
Nature abhors it
Humanity flails about it
People clean carpets

I say:
"Can't we just sit down together and
watch what happens?"

All is All
Holding All
Unfolding Now

~ J.B.

The previous exercises peek into this next section. You were asked to think about your relationship to time on a personal level (Contemplation Q*f*P 1-6) and reflect even more deeply on your life (Contemplation Q*f*P 1-7). We now begin to sketch out the map of our belonging together in time. This is not any abstract map. It is *this* map: us here together in this occasion.

REFLECTION

One's sense of separation—that I'm separate
from you and the rest of the world, so my
well-being is separate from yours—is the
fundamental delusion that needs to be overcome.

~ DAVID LOY (AMERICAN SCHOLAR AND ZEN TEACHER)

It is because of the four Radiant Forces that we belong together in time. You and I are not separate and alone. Accordingly, I have a deep desire to reach out to those who feel separate: those who are angry, hurt, lonely, or maybe even harbor negative thoughts.

If you have such feelings or thoughts, I want you to know that we are all woven together by these forces. All human beings—Homo sapiens—are made up of the same stuff at the physical level (genes, blood, brains). While no two human beings are genetically identical, the typical difference between the genomes of two individuals is less than 1% of our genetic base pairs. Our common humanity does not stop there. That gene stuff comes from someplace deeper that we all are connected to. This deeper place lies within our mammalian nervous system and in our history.

This is most obviously seen in how, as infants and throughout our lives, we learn to create a safe sense of being with and belonging with others. And this occurs through facial expressions, the tone of our voice, and the way we express our feelings toward each other. All of this comes from how the human nervous system is wired. In essence, our species has survived through love, which is how we coregulate our lives together.

The entire human species has evolved because of the four Radiant Forces: because we have lived through chaos together—in separate tribes and ethnic groups as well as an entire planet, because we have learned from each other's ability to shape time—in shared agriculture, civilization, and technology, because we have celebrated our own becoming and growth—through art, music, culture, and because we inherit traditions and routines that give us a sense of security and safety—from mother-infant bonding to family systems to laws and institutions.

A map is most useful when it calls us to a journey and then helps us share the journey with others. A map is not useful if it never leaves my back pocket. So, imagine that I have taken it out and am unfurling it with you. We may believe that we are alone—or we may even act that way. This is an illusion.

Science ever yields insights into the nature of the universe and how time functions. In this chapter on unfolding, we elaborate on four such insights: gravity, entropy, cause and effect, and self-organizing systems and the understanding that all things unfold. The four insights loosely correspond to the four choices you made in the Contemplation QfP 1-6 exercise.

First, there is gravity, a universal force that attracts one body to another, that holds things together, or at least in nearby orbit to one another. When I say, "I am holding it together," I (this ego that thinks it's in control) fail to let gravity do its job. I really don't need to hold it together. Gravity takes care of me, helps me be whole, to belong in the orbit of others. Gravity and time work together. When the force of Attraction is the strongest, time actually slows down.

But … science also acknowledges a force called entropy. All things, especially living systems—or any system that has a cycle to it—move from a state of order to disorder. Entropy also means that the amount of energy we have available for getting work done, such as for living life, is always lessening. It is a law of the universe that there is an increasing chance that randomness comes into play as time passes. The universe is running down. So, when I say, "I am holding it together," I recognize another force is pulling at me. Some even define entropy as the "arrow of time." It distinguishes the past (order) from the future (disorder). Despite them, our attractions often do not last, and we may even feel repelled by something that once attracted us.

In some ways, gravity and entropy complement one another. Sure, things may be falling apart. However, when we honor our belonging, our being together as part of a whole, things take a lot less time to fall apart. Our actual being here in this moment is a result of the interplay between attraction and dissipation. We are always just here, expanding and contracting.

There is also the law of cause and effect. An effect cannot occur before its cause. And for every action, there is an equal and opposite reaction (otherwise known as Isaac Newton's third law of motion). We have a clear sense that the actions we take now, our behaviors, don't just dissipate into a vacuum. They will have some impact on the future. Because of this law, we may think everything that happens in our life is a result of actions we have or have not taken in the past. We think that our personal story, journey, history is defined by us. Indeed, when I say, "I am holding it together," I refer to myself as being the cause, the agent, the actor that is doing the holding.

But ... science also acknowledges that human beings and all the systems we create have their own self-organizing time frames, cycles, and schedules. Things take time. There are probabilities, waves of probabilities. There are phases to all aspects of life that we cannot always control or rush. Of course, our actions matter, but we all must sleep, contend with weather and the seasons, conform or otherwise work with the institutions we are part of, and go through all kinds of life cycles. Our story is not just what we have done but also how our environment and those in it change with us and often in spite of us. When I reflect on past events that have helped me through tough times, I realize that I have been "held"—the conditions and context of my life have provided a container for my even being here.

The Four Radiant Forces

The universe is unfolding right now in real time and in amazing ways. "Force" means energy that is either a push or a pull from one object or entity to another. Human beings are entities. We influence each other. We also experience forces within this universe. These forces can be seen as tendencies in all of nature, from life on Earth to large cosmic happenings. Below, I briefly describe the four main forces.

1. Form

You sense Form, a pattern which holds and connects things. Without Form, you would not have the hands, eyes, or ears necessary to receive or be here or to even be holding or listening to this book or device, nor would you be able to glean any meaning from these words. There is a tendency throughout the entire universe for things to cohere. Things come or vibrate together into some relatively steady and recognizable pattern. Gravity is the best example of how this first force works. The arising of any mental formation also is a result of this force, whether it is curiosity, desire, emotions, memory, love, or hate. For human beings, Form is often provided by a language: through words. These words, strung together through language, create meaning. Through language, the mind detects Form. The mind also provides a forum for understanding. Right now, for example, as you read this, you receive meaning. This understanding would not be possible without you and I both having previously learned grammar, rules, logic, and order. It is through this first force that this book, these words, came together. Just by your reading this, we have created coherence together.

When have you experienced a call to order, to organize, or to bring a sense of structure to your life? Conversely, when has life become too much of a routine? Are you currently happy with a regular schedule and enjoy how much your life is organized? Do your routines fit nicely with other important people in your life? Or, is the Form and structure of your life such that you don't have many connections or intimacy?

2. Time Shaping

You intend to shape time. Just by having consciousness, you are having an effect on time. You are taking time to read this. You could be doing something else. You made a decision, a choice. You have a will, an intention. You would not be reading this if you had not taken some action. You shaped time around your reading. This second force shows us the tendency for things to act, to move on their own accord and in a particular direction toward somewhere. You are doing it right now. You are reading. Some process also is shaping up, carrying you forward. You are becoming; you are creating. Things unfold in every journey, every life, because we take action. Cause and effect: We cannot help but cause things to happen, and we see the effects of our actions. Indeed, quantum physics tells us that we influence the world just by observing it.

When have you experienced a call to take action, to make things happen, take advantage of some emergent opportunity, seize the day? Do you want to shape the future of your life by yourself? How much are you open to shaping the future with others? Is it possible to journey with someone else? Or, ultimately, are we each going solo?

3. Nurturing Conditions

You are and have been nurtured by life's conditions. The conditions in your life's journey up until this point actually led you here somehow. Consider for a minute that your own journey is a gradual unfolding of curious happenstances. Conditions have changed along the way and will change again. But right now, here you are, like a sprout just emerging from soil that was previously gardened, fed nutrients, and cared for. Conditions have ripened to the point where you picked up this book. Yes, what has happened before colors what will happen next. We have come together, we will separate, and everything will happen in between. Everything.

Sometimes we let things take their own shape. Other times, we influence, nudge, back down, work around, work through, rest, retreat, and reconnect. Eventually, we gain insight into the nuance and context of our meetings. These Nurturing Conditions, the third force, bring surprise, comedy, tragedy, irony, romance, heroism. Nurturing Conditions operate independently of Form and Time Shaping. No matter how much meaning, structure, coherence, and form we think our lives have or need, the conditions may not be right for something to occur. Similarly, we may scheme, plan, strategize, and take multiple actions to create some desired outcome. Without the right conditions, that outcome may escape our intentions.

When have you experienced life circumstances indicating that it was best to wait, let things fall into place, have more patience? Have you been waiting and waiting for something to happen, and it just seems like it never will? Do you devote more of your time to helping, caring, or nurturing others' dreams and hopes instead of fully embracing your own life? Are you open-minded enough to receive a state of bliss, success, or accomplishment?

4. Chaos

Chaos pulls, excites, interrupts, and overcomes you. All of this will end, mutate, dissipate, or simply break down. The inherent Chaos of life's impermanence is most vividly represented by death, from which there is no escape. The forum is interrupted. Our efforts are futile. Conditions may not be right for a long time, if ever. This last force makes it all so precious. What are the chances, we wonder, that we were given this life, this ability to be conscious, to have the language, to partake in this journey, this story—not alone, but together? Many philosophies, struggling with this question, point us toward enlightenment, salvation, or a call to embrace the void. Chaos also contains the operations of chance, fortune, luck, and unpredictability. Things may not break down. They may twist and turn. Our journey acquires some unique mark or tendency that tells a different story from all the rest.

When have you experienced a call to be completely creative, think outside the box, do something radically different? Has life been either so predictable or so chaotic that you feel called to either take action or slow down? Do you find yourself moving from one crisis or incident to another that takes up so much of your time that you don't really have time for yourself? Or time for others? Do you have too much drama in your life, or just the right amount of excitement?

Our Will and the Law of Change

These forces combine or hold together in our lives in two ways. First, Time Shaping is often about our *will* to influence Form. We each have a will, that faculty within our mind to select a desire from among many desires and then apply our behavior to follow the desire. We want something to happen. There is some object (Form) of our will or desire, something that we would like to have, influence, shape, or change. Time Shaping does not happen in a vacuum; it happens with reference to some future form or state of things, as imagined or intended. Most of us spend a good bit of time ruminating; we meander in an aimless way without much focus. We are not present.

Second, independent of our will, Chaos and Nurturing Conditions team up to bring about *change*. Change occurs regardless of what we may will to happen. We may think, "This happened without me or without my consent" or, "I did not want that to happen." Chaos does not happen in a vacuum. There is some "thing" that transforms, mutates, or comes into being from the seed represented in Nurturing Conditions. Life's upheavals appear chaotic, turbulent, or troubling. And something new or different, subtle or grand, emerges. It is the inherent nature of change that Chaos and Nurturing Conditions work together.

For many, the goal of a human life is to bring our *will* and *change* together. We want to change things. We hope that our actions will lead to changes that give us a sense of fulfillment, release, achievement, happiness, satisfaction. If this is what you want, I encourage you to keep at it. Alternately, when things don't go the way we want, we learn through our Soulful Capacities: Acceptance for what is, Presence to the change that is unfolding, being in Flow with it, and riding the tide of Synchronicity that is likely to unfold. This is where many Treasures lie.

Contemplation (QƒP 1-8): Unfolding or Holding

This chapter dives deeper into the four Radiant Forces and introduces or suggests several interesting ideas.

1. Humanity has evolved by navigating the four forces together. Hence, we are really not separate from each other at the most basic species level.

2. Depending on which force dominates, I am either the one who is holding or being held; I am working to keep it together, or I am always together despite my efforts.

3. Our life is made up of phases where sometimes change (unpredictability, turmoil) happens, and other times we make efforts through our will (intentions, plans). These phases unfold through the operation of the Radiant Forces.

Questions

✦ Which of these ideas is easiest for you to grasp or the one that most resonates with you?

✦ What is happening in your life, relationships, work, or society that you feel reflects these ideas?

✦ Reflect on the phase of life that is unfolding in your life now: Is it more a function of your will or of change? Are you holding it together or is the phase itself holding you?

✦ Reflect on what is happening in the world right now (global issues, emergent crises, popularized events): How is humanity tending to the forces of Chaos, Nurturing Conditions, Time Shaping, and Form?

CHAPTER 9

Wisdom

Ode to Wisdom

I prefer the word "radiant";
don't just say "a whole lotta light"

The sages' wager:
there is a whole lotta something else
going on behind the seams
that we did not even know was there

Perhaps some discernment is in order,
or, waiting for you,
or, maybe
those seams will heave, break, and
light will
just pour and pour forth.

All is All
Holding All
Unfolding Now in Light

~ J.B.

Wisdom requires a balanced perspective of time: you learn to appreciate all the forces and their relationship to each other. Indeed, research suggests that wisdom is greatest for those individuals whose view of time is more expansive than restrictive. Specifically, an expansive view allows one to gather meaning from reflecting on both the past patterns of our life as well as imagining our future self. We not only see the meaning and purpose of how events unfold in our life, but we can also enjoy reminiscing about them. We also keep a sense of humor. We stay open to what we can learn moving forward.

The real benefit from contemplating the Radiant Forces comes from seeing how they dance together. Below are examples of this dance. As you review them, consider how learning and development play a part. In these examples, as in all areas of life, we develop skills, knowledge, mastery, and wisdom as we learn both the influence of these forces and our own ability to work with them.

Wisdom is the essential process. Discerning these forces in real time teaches us a wisdom that goes beyond knowledge and skill. In each example, our own wisdom evolves from both the interplay of the forces and our appreciation of this interplay.

A person falls in love. He, she, they send messages to get their beloved's attention. Such efforts may result in courtship and eventually a long-term commitment. Alternately, those messages never obtain their effect, love may wane, or any number of things lead to the partners' separation. Sir Harold Nicolson wrote, "The great secret of successful marriages is to treat all disasters as incidents and none of the incidents as disasters."

The gardener works the soil, reading weather and season to know when to plant and harvest. Watering, tending, protecting, and weeding are needed to help plants mature. And time, storms, frosts, and unforeseen events and pests can damage or destroy all the gardener's good work.

The sailor steers the ship across the waves. This requires knowledge of the ship's structure, ocean, wind and weather currents, and navigation skills. To make progress, the sails and rudder are continually adjusted in response to changing conditions. At the same time, run-ins with weather, hidden debris, or other vessels could lead to delays or damage to the ship.

The potter or ceramicist uses clay, a potter's wheel, a variety of crafting tools, and a kiln to produce a finished piece. The potter kneads, wedges, glazes, decorates, and applies many techniques to get to the final product. At the same time, many things could go wrong—from the composition of the clay to the temperature in the kiln.

Insight (on love, gardening, sailing, pottery) comes through experiencing and recovering from the failures. We learn how to anticipate and prevent them. Most of all, wisdom comes from knowing how to work with all the emergent forces as they unfold during the process of loving, creating, and working.

	Form	Time Shaping	Nurturing Conditions	Chaos
Love	Love's phases, such as dating, commitment, engagement, marriage, divorce, remarriage, renewal of vows	Sending a message; cueing interest; scheduling a date; developing routines together	Being introduced; falling in and out of love; times when things seem to naturally work out; times when they don't; patience; impatience; tolerance; intolerance	Breakdowns in communication; an affair; jealousy; abuse; partner's disruptive behavior; death; disease
Gardening	Soil, seeds, gardening tools, gardening plot	Planting, watering, weeding, clipping, harvesting	Seasonal variations; temperature; wind; composition of soil; neighboring flora; helpful insects	Storms; excessive weather (rain, sun, heat); blight; hurtful insects; disruptive animals; thieves; illness of gardener

	Form	Time Shaping	Nurturing Conditions	Chaos
Sailing	Structure of boat from bow to stern (deck, sail, mast, rudder, keel, fore, aft, etc.); location of all tools (such as ropes, cords, anchor)	Navigation; steering; setting sail; tacking; trimming	Weather and changes in the wind and water currents; harbor traffic; teamwork and coordination of crew	Storms; excessive wind; accidents; morale or other problems with crew; shorthanded; being unprepared
Pottery	Clay; potter's wheel; kiln; tools	Gathering clay; kneading, wedging, glazing, decorating; kiln operation	Temperature and humidity; composition of clay; quality and operation of the kiln	Problems with clay, kiln, broken tools; poor design; lack of planning

In the above examples, Form can be seen in the relationships *between* (the two partners: the garden and gardener, the boat and the sailor, the pottery and the potter). Time shaping occurs *in* (flirting and dating, planting and weeding, navigating and adjusting, kneading and firing). The right timing and facilitative factors of Nurturing Conditions are required for results *from* (the relationship to connect and endure: the flower, fruit or vegetable to ripen and find its way to the kitchen, the boat to dock safely in the harbor, or the clay to transform into a utensil a family uses for generations). And Chaos, perhaps the most obvious, can intervene at any point to interfere *with* (a visit from an ex, a summer drought, a mutiny, or a crack in the kiln).

Contemplation (QfP 1-9): Wisdom

Reflect on a current life challenge or stressor (emotions, work, relationship). Consider the current situation. How have previous conditions led to it? What role do your actions play now? What factors lie outside your control or are unpredictable?

After you reflect on these questions, rate yourself on the items below that represent having wisdom from and about that area of your life.

	Disagree	Neutral	Agree
I have a sense of humor or see irony about the situation.			X
I remain open-minded about the meaning and outcome.			X
I sense my stress will subside, or "this too shall pass."			✓
I can see myself looking back at the situation and gaining a sense of growth or understanding from it.			✓
I recognize that my situation is part of a larger set of circumstances designed to help me grow or learn.			✓

It's a deep cleansing --- removing from my life that which no longer serves me.

Discernment

Ode to Discernment

My eyes squeeze tight to catch a glint

There are two things on the horizon:
Death and that which is possible, and
Life and that which is impossible

The light changes and I squint again
Another two things:
A murmuration of birds as they swirl
   around a mountain
A long shafting waterfall in that mountain

And the light plays again:
And there You Are
Right in front of me The Whole Time
Squinting back at me
and smiling

~ J.B.

Unlike previous chapters, this chapter provides four distinct contemplations. First, I provide a brief definition of the force. Second, I offer a reflection from my own life. Then, I provide commentary to bring the ideas back to you and me. Finally, I provide questions to help you focus on how the force operates in your life right now, at this instant.

Discernment is the application of both intention and attention together. Our growth on the quest for presence quickens when we discriminate how the forces manifest in our lives. Even though they dance together (see previous chapter), the forces also show up in distinct ways. Cultivating discernment is a spiritual practice, a practice that we can do together.

At the beginning of this book, I suggested that we best appreciate our time with each other. By "each other," I meant you and others in your life who you may share this book with but also you (as the reader) and me. I also hoped you would get to know me well enough so, whatever your objectives, you feel less alone and more connected.

If you have read through to here, you and I are somehow more connected through time. More importantly, you recognize that we (all of us, humanity together) have the whole time been going through the dance of this happening life with the four forces.

Form

Definition. Form encompasses all and anything that brings cohesion and alignment to the occasion, the situation, the routine you have with others. In daily life, this includes the waking and sleeping cycle and the various rituals and routines in between. In culture and civilization, Form manifests as rules for communicating, coordinating activities, working, mating, and persisting and evolving through time. Form also manifests as maintaining, or agreeing to maintain, some shape that is recognized by society as a way of being, a recognizable social form (con-**form**-ity), from local social norms to global culture.

REFLECTION

At the start of this book, I described my childhood experience of becoming intensely aware of death as a sense of complete and utter void, and the reality that "I" will die. When I shared this with my parents, they told me to just ignore it and go back to bed. Since then, I have had other experiences where I sensed that there is something beyond my own "I" that is part and parcel of all matter and energy. The "I" of my childhood terror was really an attachment to an idea: I am separate from others and the world. Perhaps I would have fared better if my parents had been more consoling. A part of me would have liked to have heard, "Yes, it is terrifying. We are all going to die. But don't worry about it because we, your Mommy and Daddy, are here to help you figure it out and support you as you grow." Another part of me is grateful that the experience unfolded as it did. That's because, at least for a short while, I was consoled by the notion that the frightening permanence of death might one day simply stop being a concern. While I came away with an initial sense that everything that appears to have a lasting or permanent form will eventually and simply vanish, the seed of Acceptance for the formless was planted.

I don't blame my parents. They did their best. In sharing my experience with others, I have felt less alone. The fear of death is universal. Also, I had this experience before I had any knowledge of religion or of stories about life after death. I believe that this has made me more open-minded about how we, humanity, throughout history, have devised various solutions to death.

What does my childhood experience have to do with Form? It made me aware of how much I yearned to have some concrete image, some person to hold on to. Later in life, this manifested as extreme possessiveness, jealousy, and addictive actions in my close relationships.

Seen through the lens of religion, the experience made me aware of how easily people can worship idols or leaders. A blind need for security leads them to become rigidly attached to one way of thinking: a political party, a theory, a fundamentalist dogma, one single and only true religion. Objectively, Form by itself doesn't breed or create attachment. Rather, it is our overidentification with, obsession with, or single-minded focus on a particular Form (meaning idol worship).

It is important to distinguish the general idea of the *force* of Form from the specific manifestation of Form in our lives. My experience was my initial awareness of how much we, as human beings, are strongly driven to establish meaning, coherence, and togetherness with something or someone outside our own skin.

This universal force leads to the creation of a rich variety of relationship Forms: family, friendship, romantic, casual, intimate, legal, transactional, political, and so forth. Another is like between an author and reader. Between you and me. Now.

> **Questions:** How is the force of Form operating right now as you read or listen to this? What is the shape, texture, or Form of our relationship—as author and reader—and how is it maintaining itself or changing right now? How has it changed over time?

TIME SHAPING

Definition. Time Shaping is any action or process of taking an action. The tension or new opportunity that results when a living system forms an intention (desire, need, or impulse) can be realized only by taking the other forces (Chaos, Nurturing Conditions, and Form) into account. This is shown in behavior *toward* an end-state (telos)—molting, mounting, and molding—that occurs with others in a shared ecosystem. Time Shaping materializes in all creativity, fabrication, linearity. It contains the memory of each element and the trajectory for that element. The future is made real through Time Shaping.

REFLECTION

My awareness of death and my initial interest in studying spirituality were somehow tied to my relationship with my maternal grandmother, "Nanny," who had lost her husband years before. Nanny lived about a mile away, and I often would ride the bus or walk to her apartment on Friday afternoons after school. In observance of the Jewish Sabbath, Nanny would light candles and would prohibit me from flipping on light switches on Saturdays.

My weekend visits to Nanny increased around the time of my parents' divorce when I was twelve and continued for several years after my bar mitzvah. I was not an obedient student in Hebrew school, yet I learned to sing my bar mitzvah reading directly from the Hebrew Torah. I remember getting up before dawn and walking to the synagogue by myself to prepare with the morning minyan of ten older men. At the time, I felt that this was a real initiation, a "coming of age," for two reasons. First, I was preparing and singing on my own within the loving presence of these men in a holy space. I had, within Jewish tradition, done it by myself. Second, my parents' divorce was still fresh and traumatic for everyone. This was 1968, and my family was the first in our neighborhood to have experienced divorce. The bar mitzvah was conducted on a Thursday morning, with only the minyan and my family, partly due to cost but also because the divorce was too "raw" to have the ceremony in the larger synagogue setting. I was initiated into a protected space. The bar mitzvah was a haven, separate from the drama in my family and the sense of shame that we could not hold it together.

Throughout high school, I continued to visit Nanny, and I would bring my books to study and write over the weekend. I began studying different religions and purchased a Penguin Books copy of *The Bhagavad Gita* that included verses from the Upanishads. I wrote a book report in school and began talking about these ideas with friends. Because my friends knew my interest, I was invited to attend a meeting to learn about a guru whose practices were based in *The Bhagavad Gita*. Within a few weeks, I got a ride to attend an initiation weekend where I first learned meditation techniques. I was fifteen years old.

Rites of passage or initiation ceremonies exist in every culture. Even when social norms deteriorate and such rituals fray, young, emerging adults find some type of activity (through hazing, drugs, alcohol, or other high-risk behavior) to prove themselves, show that they are resilient, invincible, invulnerable, or transcendent. All such acts have the quality of making a mark, setting out on a journey, and shaping the future.

This time of life—emerging adulthood, the transition from adolescence to adulthood—is the most emblematic of Time Shaping in the course of our development. The brain goes through tremendous changes as we find our direction and negotiate hormonal expressions, our family of origin "home space," educational requirements, and the trials of entering the world of work. It is also a time of novelty and creativity, two factors that fuel and instigate Time Shaping. Partly because of this fuel, Time Shaping happens at all phases of life. We retain the ability to keep learning and changing, even in older age. We can continually find or cultivate novelty and creativity as we age.

Digging deeper into Time Shaping, we may uncover insight into our soul's longer journey, our reason for being here. The dreams we have as emerging adults—dreams of accomplishment, success, love, family—can inspire us but also limit us. The path we thought we were set upon may not be the real path of our calling or legacy. Our sense of duty may be a gradual awakening. We start to see how our past actions led us to this moment of taking "right" or resonant actions in our lives. There are so many strands in our life story, our past … our karma. Any one of them might pull us to take action in ways we could not anticipate: a sudden decision, a chance encounter, a disruptive dream, an illness. For me, meditation and prayer led to outcomes that changed the direction of my life.

This is a core principle about Time Shaping: The act and discipline of meditation or prayer (or any intentional spiritual practice) are how we can renew our sacred sense of time. Every religious or spiritual tradition encourages, guides, and gives recurrent opportunities for meditation, prayer, or some "time set aside" from all other "worldly" routines. Not only is time set aside, so is place. The word *temple* comes from the same language roots as the words *time* and *template*. (I delve into this further in Book 2).

In Time Shaping, we cut, demarcate, divide, or segment the overall and continuous unfolding of our life: this happening life. And so, a rite of passage is about *passing* from one segment of our life to another: just as the sabbath was given special separateness, just as our passage into old age and from this life into whatever lies next, and just as you're taking time out to read this now.

Questions: How is Time Shaping operating right now as you read or listen to this? What actions are you taking in response to the actions I took in writing this down? Did a particular exercise or contemplation prompt you? What future actions might you take?

NURTURING CONDITIONS

Definition. Also known as *facilitative conditions* or *supportive context*, Nurturing Conditions reflect the idea that everything—especially our relationship with ourself and with others—becomes or ripens into its next phase of existence or evolution. Everything has its own time. There is a waiting time, a growing time, and a coming-into-its-own time. This is most deeply witnessed with a patient, humble silence that embraces both the grand and tiny unfoldments in life with compassion. Nurturing Conditions are revealed in knowing when the time is "right" (meant to be) or when things are aligned for either coming together, being apart, or a true being "just with."

REFLECTION

What if everything that happens in life is designed to teach us? I was sixteen or seventeen when I first experienced what I later learned were "out-of-body" episodes. I believe these stemmed, at least in part, from meditation. I would come home from school and nap in the late afternoon. On several occasions, I would enter some type of trance and experience my entire being lifting out of the body, while at the same time feeling a struggle to stay in the body. This dual tension led to a feeling of paralysis and heart pounding. Feeling starkly anxious, I flailed my arms and fists to beat the side of the bed to wake up.

The out-of-body experiences and readings about consciousness led me on a search and into a series of encounters with remarkable people, teachers, therapists, and mentors who nourished me in ways for which I will feel forever grateful. These teachers and supporters have always appeared at the right time in my life. Some were very special.

At about the time of the out-of-body experiences, I was a child-care worker for children with special needs, which included autism, childhood schizophrenia, and one unique teenager who had received a prefrontal lobotomy. I believe administrators entrusted me with these children because I had a way of communicating that encouraged the children to open up to me. It is hard to explain in words, but we had empathy for each other, and they taught me greatly about being in the moment—moment to moment.

I was responsible for giving "my kids" their medication. I was educated on the pharmacological effects and knew that the drugs had to be strictly regulated and protected. However, I had a growing concern because I could tell that after taking these drugs, my kids would become different people—zombies, flat, apart, not connected. My concern for them, along with my own teenage impulsivity, propelled my decision to take a dose of one of the drugs—Thorazine (chlorpromazine).

The Thorazine led to significant drowsiness followed by almost two days of sleep. During this time, all the staff, other childcare workers, and counselors met to decide whether I should be fired. Fortunately, one senior counselor took me under his wing, and I was allowed to stay on for another full year until I left for college.

Nurturing Conditions pulse constantly in the background and support all that is. Attuning to them, we experience life most fully. In the metaphors described earlier (love, gardening, sailing, pottery), we can develop sensitivity to factors that facilitate growth, maturation, or fulfillment. Wisdom comes when we learn *within* these conditions (full immersion) rather than trying to control or master them.

Of course, it helps to know the right time to kiss, the best conditions for planting in soil, the ideal weather and currents for sailing, and so on. But life is organic, dynamic, and fluctuating. Conditions, and the actions we take within those conditions, do not always appear to align. We act on impulse and intuition, and we experiment. We take chances. Sometimes others catch us if we fall. Sometimes not. And yet, as the pattern of our life plays out—if we allow life to teach us—we can discern that all experiences occur amid and within a supportive context. There are no accidents.

Both science and philosophy validate the existence of Nurturing Conditions. Scientists who study cosmology—the science of the origin and development of the entire universe—believe that dark matter accounts for 80% of all matter in the universe, even though physicists cannot detect dark matter with current methods. The primary evidence lies in calculations showing that without this unseeable matter, galaxies would fly apart, they would not rotate, or they would have never formed in the first place. Dark matter is the infrastructure or latticework that allows that which can be seen to exist.

As we discussed previously, a core principle in Taoist philosophy is the Tao itself. Tao literally translates into "the way," and within the practice and philosophy of Taoism, Tao is meant to connote nature or the way to return to our original and essential nature through a guiding intelligence, an intimate divine presence, or related term (the Source, the Nameless Simplicity, the Original Ancestor). Many of the teachings of Taoism claim that it cannot be seen, named, or even described with words. Yet it is everywhere; it can only be experienced directly, and it makes up our ordinary daily life and routines.

According to the Taoist philosopher Lao Tzu, "The best teacher is the one of whom the students are not even aware." When the task is accomplished, and everything is complete, the students will say, "We did it all by ourselves." As life has happened, many teachers—people, situations, events—have supported my growth. My sincere hope is that this book and your reading of it brings you to the insight that Nurturing Conditions are happening right this instant. Experience them as deeply as you can. Drink them in. Now.

> **Questions:** How is the force of Nurturing Conditions operating right now as you read or listen to this? What is coming into being as a result of my writing and you reading this? How is it bringing us both back, in accordance with the Tao, to our essential nature? What new context or new set of conditions are evolving that would not have evolved if it were not for this writing and your reading?

CHAOS

Definition. Chaos is the living process of coming apart, breaking up, and the murky, unpredictable, distorted, and uncontrollable response to this process. Chaos is revealed in the rawness of pain and the dark emotions—unbridled rage, panic, arresting anxiety, depression's gloom, frantic jealousy— or in the suddenness of events, accidents, turbulence, catastrophe, and the unpredictable bifurcation of a life path. Chaos is hidden but always lurking, influencing the ordinary, the calm, the mundane.

REFLECTION

We are all brushed with Chaos: cut, thrust, broken, falling. I was standing at the top of the stairs at age five. My mother winced at me being a pest, jealous for attention, tugging at her leg. I fell down a full flight, accusing, screaming, rageful. Then, at age ten, I was in the kitchen with Nanny, who accidentally spilled a pot of boiling water on my back when I ran into her in a hyperactive spree. Then, my father was slapping me in the face, bringing me back into consciousness and out of the hysterical in searing pain. Here are other fragments from childhood.

I was playing with my brother in our room when the dresser fell down, trapping both of us. I remember hiding under the bed at different times growing up, the first in fear of the boogeyman, then later out of fear of everything falling apart. My parents fighting, breaking dishes, one of them screaming, "I am going to get a gun." Later, seeing the first gaping hole in the living room wall from my father's fist of rage. And the second hole after he plastered over the first. Then him coming home drunk with his hand broken after he slammed his fist into the metal door at work. My father's crazy driving, threatening to kill us all. Being bullied and beat up at school.

Later, in junior high school, I had these sudden and sharp surges of desire, of longing, of being spontaneously overrun with emotion for a girl I fell in love with. Inexplicably being overwhelmed with the constant need to be with her and, simultaneously, keeping that need a sacred secret. Feeling possessed. And more screaming and fighting at home. Waking up every morning, sometime in my teens, with a dread: free-floating anxiety, with no anchor, somewhere in the vast pit of my stomach. Then, acting out impulsively. Throwing a book at my chaperone, my den mother, and being kicked out of the Cub Scouts. Taking bathroom breaks in school and pulling the fire alarm. Running away. Hiding. Hiding on the beach.

My mother's drinking, smoking, overeating. Her deterioration and heart attack and death at an early age. No one in the family came to support me, my brother, and Nanny burying my mother. Shame. Despair. Meaninglessness. Continued morning anxiety well until my thirties.

Somehow, one day in my college dorm room, I kicked in and broke a door out of a deep, uncontrollable jealousy and possessiveness of my girlfriend. Suicidal images. In that instant, I knew it was time to get help.

Please do not compare my experience of pain with yours. We all have our own version of "I am hurting." We need to be reminded that we are never alone in our pain. The human mind can only tolerate so much pain, deterioration, disease, death ... Chaos. And yet, Chaos is inevitably woven into everything.

We both avoid and also court Chaos. In my story, some of the Chaos I describe is self-inflicted, born out of impatience, impulsiveness, and lack of self-regulation. We know Chaos when we know what is uncontrollable in our lives. The "Serenity Prayer" reveals this: "God grant me the serenity to accept the things I cannot change."

Chaos often gives us insight into the larger sense of time and an enduring quality that transcends our own human experience. This is revealed in many inspirational and wise quotes about pain, suffering, adversity, hard times, and death. Every aphorism on adversity or Chaos denotes the sense of potential or of movement into a future. The difficulty gives birth to a new possibility, if not "a multiplicity of possibilities."

Consider just these few:

If you want the rainbow, you gotta put up with the rain.
~ DOLLY PARTON (AMERICAN SINGER-SONGWRITER)

Don't cry over spilled milk. By this time
tomorrow it will be free yogurt.
~ STEPHEN COLBERT (AMERICAN COMEDIAN
AND POLITICAL COMMENTATOR)

One must still have chaos in oneself to be
able to give birth to a dancing star.
~ FRIEDRICH NIETZSCHE (GERMAN PHILOSOPHER)

Chaos is inherent in all compounded
things. Strive on with diligence.
~ THE BUDDHA

Chaos does not mean total disorder. Chaos means a
multiplicity of possibilities. Chaos is from the ancient
Greek word that means a thing that is birthed from the void.
And it was about that which is possible, not about disorder.

~ JOK CHURCH (AMERICAN CARTOONIST)

Obviously, rain, spilled milk, chaos, and disorder are inherent parts of life. Suffering need not result from these experiences. It is how we get caught up in the sensations—the momentary capture of the experiences—that leads to suffering. The Buddha also says, "Pain is inevitable. Suffering is optional."

Hence, Chaos is often the greatest teacher of time as well as timelessness. There is an aspect of our humanness that transcends the sensations associated with Chaos. This "self-transcendence" was described by Abraham Maslow as a move beyond self-actualization. It is more than our current identity, our personality, our preferences. It is more enduring. Various names have been used: our essence, our essential nature, our core of being, our higher nature, our ultimate beingness, our "Real Self." It also has been called our soul.

Ultimately, Chaos forces us to embrace our humanness and to transcend our own limited self in doing so. We are part of a common humanity that we can serve. As I have said, this is my main reason for writing to you. I certainly cannot do this alone. Perhaps in my sharing, I can be of service. I hope my own story helps you to get in touch with your own story, to embrace it, to transcend it. We can do this together. Now.

Questions: How is the force of Chaos operating right now as you read or listen to this? What is being opened, interrupted, or thrown off course to reveal some essential vulnerability, unknown, or human brokenness? How can you feel less alone by knowing I have experienced some aspect of this same Chaos?

Contemplation (QfP 1-10): Pause

Take a moment to pause and reflect on everything we have covered regarding the four Radiant Forces.

In chapter 1, before learning anything about them, you were asked to rate which one was at the forefront of your life right now.

In chapter 5, as part of the Time Adjustment Protocol, you were introduced to the idea that the forces represent objective reality, that they can manifest as unhelpful mental states, and that spiritual practices can help us get in touch with them.

Chapter 6 reminded us that the forces are not really separate, and they all work together as a totality, a unified whole, just as a map, tapestry, or mandala is a single whole. Contemplation 6 in chapter 6 asked you to rank order your preference for different views on the passage of time.

Chapter 8 offered a broader perspective on the forces. You were encouraged to view them as the unfolding of life events and were prompted with many questions to help you see the role of the forces in your life, past and present.

In this last chapter, I shared a succinct definition and personal story about each force. I am trying to prompt you to reflect on how each force operates in your life right now. This last contemplation asks you to think about why you are asked to do all this reflection. To summarize:

+ The forces operate as a whole, and some come to the forefront of your attention at any given moment or phase of your life.

+ The forces show up in your mental states.

+ You can touch upon and work with them through spiritual practice.

+ You may have a preference for different forces.

- Everything that happens—indeed, your whole sense that life *is* happening—is a function of the forces working together.

- You will benefit from seeing how the forces operate in your life to shape your story or journey to the Treasures.

- In this very moment, as you read or listen to this, the forces are at work.

- You gain wisdom by making the effort to witness them in this moment.

Questions:

- What benefit is there to contemplating and discerning the forces?

- Return to your first response to Contemplation QfP 1-1 (end of chapter 1). There, you were encouraged to review each of the five quick self-assessments in chapter 1 (the four Radiant Forces, the four Soulful Capacities, etc.). Assuming that now you have more time to review the four Radiant Forces, what has changed? What do you now notice about your own understanding of these forces and the role they play in your life?

- Finally, consider these lines below as a repetition, mantra, or prayer. Find a space and time to silently and slowly repeat these lines. Notice how your awareness changes while doing so:

All is All

Holding All

Unfolding Now in Light

Additional Treasures

The sixteen Treasures described in QfP were derived from my personal study of the Soulful Capacities, the Radiant Forces, and their intersection. I labeled those Treasures to capture a distinct variety but make no claims the list is comprehensive. Three other approaches to Treasures are described here. The authors use other terms—"Spiritual Principles" (Connie Kaplan), "Being Values" (Abraham Maslow), and "Spiritual Practices" (Frederic and Mary Ann Brussat). In providing their lists below, I hope to not misrepresent their approaches, and I encourage you to consult the original sources.

As you review the lists, you may notice some commonalities (for example, Beauty, Love, Play) and differences. You also might notice commonalities and differences in comparison with the sixteen Treasures. Hopefully, you will clearly see that there is an abundance of experiences that are possible in this precious weave. Treasure on!

30 Spiritual Principles (Kaplan)		17 Being Values (Maslow)	37 Spiritual Practices (The Brussats)	
Kaplan claims that these metaphysical principles weave together to create our human experience of the world. While we work with all thirty principles, each person is connected in a unique way with a few of them. Kaplan's work is to help you learn your unique pattern.		Abraham Maslow claims that these are ideal, ultimate, and unanalyzable attributes of reality that are perceived in peak experiences.	Frederic and Mary Ann Brussat claim these practices are key elements of religions and spirituality movements. On their website, the Brussats claim that these practices "help us discover our deepest values, address our longing to connect with the divine, and propel us on the journey to wholeness."	
www.theinvisiblegarment.com		www.maslow.com	www.spiritualityandpractice.com	
placement	resistance	truth	attention	meaning
innocence	unity	goodness	beauty	nurturing
purity	attraction	beauty	being present	openness
memory	focus	wholeness	compassion	peace
beauty	service	dichotomy- transcendence	connections	play
extension	gratitude		devotion	questing
regeneration	harmony	aliveness	enthusiasm	reverence
generosity	dreaming	uniqueness	faith	shadow
goodness	randomness	perfection	forgiveness	silence
awareness	humility	necessity	grace	teachers
reciprocity	desire	completion	gratitude	transformation
flowering	silence	justice	hope	unity
creativity	peace	order	hospitality	vision
intelligence	love	simplicity	imagination	wonder
ecstasy	movement	richness	joy	x–the mystery
		effortlessness	justice	yearning
		playfulness	kindness	you
		self-sufficiency	listening	zeal
			love	

Readings on Time Beyond Time

These five different readings are contemplations on time. Taken together, they can be considered the first or the last of all the contemplation exercises in the entire QfP collection (that is, including all five books). Read through them and share and study with others. Explore their common message and their differences. Use them to have conversations with those whose faith or persuasion is different from yours.

1. Atheism

Know that the world will outlive you.
How you live your life will affect others,
whether or not you are around to know it.
You want to be the kind of person
who has the larger view,
who takes other's interests into account,
who's dedicated to principles you can justify
like justice,
knowledge,
truth,
beauty
and morality.

~ ADAPTED FROM STEVEN PINKER, COGNITIVE PSYCHOLOGIST AND ATHEIST (FROM *A BETTER LIFE: 100 ATHEISTS SPEAK OUT ON JOY & MEANING IN A WORLD WITHOUT GOD* BY CHRIS JOHNSON)

2. Old Testament

Show me, O Lord, my life's end,
and the number of my days;
let me know how fleeting is my life.

My life is a handbreadth
  before thee ...

We are but phantoms going to and fro;
heaping up all kinds of wealth;
never knowing where
it will all go.

~ PSALM OF DAVID (PSALMS 39:4-6;
  ADAPTED FROM NIV)

3. New Testament

Consider the lilies of the field,
they neither toil nor spin,

Yet I tell you, even Solomon in
  all his glory was not arrayed
  like one of these ...

Therefore, do not be anxious, saying, 'What shall we eat?'
  or 'What shall we drink?' or 'What shall we wear? ...

do not be anxious about tomorrow, for tomorrow will be
  anxious for itself.

Sufficient for the day is its own trouble.

~ JESUS CHRIST (MATTHEW 6:28-34; ADAPTED FROM ESV)

4. Buddhism

Thus, shall ye think of all this
fleeting world ...

a star at dawn
a bubble in a stream
a flash of lightning in a summer cloud
a flickering lamp,
a phantom,
and a dream.

~ THE BUDDHA (DIAMOND SUTRA)

5. Islam

I swear by the time
(the evening tide),
Everyone is in a state of loss,
Except those who believe
and do good and
join together in truth,
patience, and constancy.

~ THE HOLY QUR'AN (ADAPTED)
(CHAPTER 103: AL-ASR; THE EVENTIDE)

Note. These, and other readings, are presented as a Contemplation in the preview to QfP: *The Connoisseur of Time: An Invitation to Presence.* You can download this from our website at no cost. Please visit www.presencequest.life.

Key Terms

Attractions (see Book 3). The nine Attractions are aspects of our personality and represent personal tendencies that each individual has toward one or more of the four Radiant Forces. Attractions show us how our particular attitudes, moods, motives, and strengths move (pull, draw, invite) us from our current state of being to a deeper, more essential or soulful state. When in this state, we are more in touch with the Radiant Forces from which the Attractions are born. The nine Attractions are Catalyzing, Intending, Coordinating, Centering, Discerning, Potentiating, Crafting, Opening, and Synthesizing.

Chaos (also entropy, dissolution). One of the four Radiant Forces, Chaos represents an objective reality: everything is in a state of disintegration. We glimpse Chaos in experiences of impermanence, disorder, randomness, challenges, disruption, the unknown. As an objective reality, there is nothing inherently negative or evil in Chaos. That which is wild, untamed, or chaotic may hold as much value as that which is steady, tamed, and orderly. When Chaos is active in our lives, we are often called to be creative.

Clock-time. As used in QfP, clock-time refers to the earth-bound physical and mechanical device that is: (1) used to measure time for a social or public group, (2) in order for that group to keep track of time, and (3) as a way to introduce order in reference to the roughly twenty-four-hour day of the earth's rotational cycle. There are other types of clocks, such as a biological clock that refers to hormonal and other body cycles and a psychological clock that refers to our own internal sense of time. From the perspective of the human species, physical and mechanical clock-time is relative and subjective; it is an idiosyncratic artifice of measuring time because of the earth's axis and rotation in reference to the sun. Clock-time on another planet would be entirely different. In QfP, we attempt to understand clock-time as objectively as possible and without negative judgment. It is sometimes referred to as small t time or time on the surface in comparison to a big T time, a more comprehensive view of time that is deeper and more important for being and presence.

Contemplation. Contemplation is both a verb and a noun in Quest for Presence and has two meanings: 1) The act of looking thoughtfully at something for a long time, and 2) Exercises (located at the end of each chapter) designed to encourage you to engage with the concepts presented, noticing them at work in your life.

Form (also structure, organization). One of the four Radiant Forces, Form represents an objective reality: everything has a shape, a recognizable pattern, integrity, or coherence. We glimpse Form in experiences of order, regularity, rules, routines, security, organizations, institutions. As an objective reality, there is nothing inherently positive or good about Form. When Form is active in our lives, we are often called to order.

Mandala. A mandala is both an image and a principle. As an image, it has been defined by Random House Webster's Collegiate Dictionary (1992) as a "concentric configuration of geometric shapes, each of which contains an image or attribute of a deity." The mandala originates from Buddhist and Hindu philosophy as a schematized representation of the cosmos. The spiritual and philosophical aspects of mandalas are overlooked, often due to commercial representations. In Quest for Presence, the mandala principle refers to the idea of orderly mayhem: that everything we experience has interdependence—a center has its fringe and vice versa.

Nurturing Conditions (this can go by other terms, such as temporal context, becoming, facilitative conditions, cooperating cause, concurrent conditions, circumstantial conditions, nutritive cause). One of the four Radiant Forces, Nurturing Conditions represent an objective reality: everything is in the process of unfolding, becoming, coming into being or transitioning from one form to the next. We glimpse Nurturing Conditions in processes—such as the experiences of waiting, arriving, growing, decaying—and in current state or circumstance—such as harmony or disharmony, fit or unfit, time to leave or time to stay. As an objective reality, there is no value to be placed on Nurturing Conditions. When it is active in our lives, we are often called to wait, listen, discern, and align.

Precious Weave. This is a central metaphor in Quest for Presence. As a noun, the weave refers to the interconnections between all the elements discussed: moments, occasions, Radiant Forces, Soulful Capacities, Attractions, Treasures, and Trajectories. When used as a noun, the synonymous term *tapestry* would suffice. However, as a verb, the precious weave conveys that these interconnections are dynamic, ever-changing, and experienced as something of great value.

Presence. One of the four Soulful Capacities (see Book 2), Presence refers to being centered in the moment and having the ability to be fully attentive to oneself and one's environment with a sense of aliveness, full engagement, and attunement to the moment with heart and mind.

Radiant Forces. These underlying energy sources form the basis of the precious weave. It is through their existence and interaction that we experience the world, and specifically, time, as we do. Everything that we recognize as happening emerges or unfolds through the activity of these four forces. Each force itself is energy and has strength with the potential to move things, influence, and provide power to our awareness. Our experience of time's flow (moving from past to present to future) also depends upon the operation and interaction of each force. These forces exist independent of our experience, but we would not experience any part of our happening life without them.

Soulful Capacity (see Book 2). A Soulful Capacity is our innate and ever-present ability to experience the precious weave and the operation of the Radiant Forces, especially as those forces manifest in the Treasures of this happening life. Quest for Presence identifies four such capacities: Acceptance, Presence, Flow, and Synchronicity. They are soulful because they come from and help us touch a more enduring, essential, and transcendent experience of our journey in this life.

Tao. *Tao* or *dao* is a Chinese word meaning the way, path, route, or road. In Chinese philosophy, Tao is the absolute principle underlying the universe, combining within itself the principles of yin and yang and signifying the way, or code of behavior, that is in harmony with the natural order.

This Happening Life. The term "happening" refers to an event or occurrence that is taking place or in process in the current moment or occasion. Hence, this life is itself a happening or is always in a state of process, emergence, or unfolding.

Time. The definition of time in standard American English typically refers to (a) the *perceived* or apparent distinction between past, present, and future; (b) the sense that there is directionality from past to future; and (c) the sense that there is this moment (now) and the sense of duration of that now. These definitions indicate that time is entirely subjective. From the viewpoint of modern physics, cosmology, and quantum mechanics, there is no such thing as an objective reality of time. And yet, a review of many definitions within the *Oxford English Dictionary* reveals many ways that we use time to navigate our seeming reality. This includes time as in a clock (clock-time), a continuity, a system of recording hours, a time available, a particular period of time for which something is happening (holiday time, time for bed), a particular point in the day, an occasion, a period in history (times gone by; times have changed). The dictionary also references time as in a race (the number of minutes, hours, seconds to complete a sprint, a leg, or a marathon), as in music (the number of beats in a measure, the speed [tempo] at which it is intended to be played), and as in the length of a criminal's exile in prison ("doing time").

Time Shaping. One of the four Radiant Forces, Time Shaping represents an objective reality where one entity or object has an influence or impact on other entities with regard to how an event or events turn out. We understand Time Shaping through intentionality, desire, or will and the subsequent behaviors that follow the intention. It also shows up in purpose, objectives, goal-oriented behaviors, expectations, work, tasks, iterations, and patterns of activity that reveal cause and effect. As an objective reality, there is no value to be placed on Time Shaping or intentions. When it is active in our lives, we are often called to take action, make a decision to select and exhibit one behavior over another, or pursue a series of acts.

Trajectories (see Book 4). A trajectory is the path followed by an object moving under the action of a given force or set of forces. In Quest for Presence, the Trajectories refer to eight ways we experience time in our day-to-day life. Each Trajectory rises to and plays out on the surface of our happening life, emerging through the interplay of the Radiant Forces operating at a deeper level. Trajectories include Routine, Scheduling, Transition, Timing, Rhythm, Transcendence, Interruption, and Pacing.

Treasures (see Book 5). A treasure is an experience—a state of consciousness—wherein one directly witnesses the value or preciousness of life as it is happening and in a way that brings a sense of uplift, wholeness, transcendence, insight, intimacy, deep perception, or some combination of these qualities. In Quest for Presence, the Treasures alter our sense of time; we become more present. The Treasures are not "out there" in the future. Treasures occur at the intersection of the Soulful Capacities and the Radiant Forces. The sixteen Treasures discussed are Spontaneity, Momentousness, Fulfillment, Clutch, Optimism, Effortlessness, Ordinariness, Coherence, Adoration, Resonance, Patience, Preciousness, Savoring, Poignance, Release, and Awe.

Whole-time. Whole-time is the sense or perspective of our whole life and experience—past, present, and future—as one seamless and ongoing whole. Our attention is not directed to the present moment any more or less than to the past or future. We have an immediate and intuitive sense of our life, our self, and our "time here" as one whole. In Quest for Presence, we sense whole-time through each of the Radiant Forces in distinctive ways; through Time Shaping we see our lifetime as one project for the realization of purpose, meaning, values, principles, and others; through Nurturing Conditions we sense we are ever becoming as part of the unfolding of humanity, history, Divine Will, or other universal force; through Chaos we see how all the apparent accidents, mishaps, twists of fate, are all part of one meaningful display along with everything else: the parts in the whole and the whole in the parts; through Form, we see how we and every experience or encounter fits together into a pattern. Overall, then, whole-time is our life as one unfolding project as glimpsed in meaning and pattern.

Research Notes

CHAPTER 1

(page 6) Regarding research on time urgency. Burnout, stress, and time urgency are all related. Research suggests that the extensive pressures and structure of workplaces have a direct cause on these problems as they lessen well-being and increase disease (Pfeffer, 2018). While this book, by itself, may not help you (by yourself) change your workplace, it provides many guides and tools to reorient you toward time in a more healthful way. Time urgency is a complex topic, involving contributions from one's personality, the standard length and pace of work in one's job, and the pace of life within a culture. Other factors related to time-urgency are hurriedness, impatience, irritability, and a compressed sense of time passing. All of these are part of the "Type A" behavior style, which has been found to correlate with greater susceptibility to cardiovascular risk, health problems, stress, and difficulty with sleep. However, the relationship between Type A and health risk may be influenced by any number of factors, including gender, occupation, and the pace and normative lifestyle of one's surrounding culture. All factors held equal, those who work long hours and have less work-life balance experience less overall psychological well-being. This relationship is exacerbated when more of the following factors occur: Type A leanings, overwork, workload, increased demands as a caregiver to children and aging parents, and the culture applying pressure to achieve, work, and be perfect. The latter – a workaholic culture of time pressure – may be the most significant contributor to time urgency and burn-out.

Cole, S. R., Kawachi, I., Liu, S., Gaziano, J. M., Manson, J. E., Buring, J. E., & Hennekens, C. H. (2001). Time urgency and risk of non-fatal myocardial infarction. *International Journal of Epidemiology, 30*(2), 363–369. https://doi.org/10.1093/ije/30.2.363

Conte, J. M., Schwenneker, H. H., Dew, A. F., & Romano, D. M. (2001). Incremental validity of time urgency and other type A subcomponents in predicting behavioral and health criteria. *Journal of Applied Social Psychology, 31*(8), 1727–1748. https://doi.org/10.1111/j.1559-1816.2001.tb02748.x

Espnes, G. A., & Byrne, D. (2016). Type A behavior and cardiovascular disease. In M. Alvarenga & D. Byrne (Eds.), *Handbook of Psychocardiology* (pp. 645–664). Springer. https://doi.org/10.1007/978-981-287-206-7_30

Gallacher, J. E. J., Sweetnam, P. M., Yarnell, J. W. G., Elwood, P. C., & Stansfeld, S. A. (2003). Is type A behavior really a trigger for coronary heart disease events? *Psychosomatic Medicine, 65*(3), 339–346. https://doi.org/10.1097/01.PSY.0000041608.55974.A8

Kamphuis, R. (2018). *Using stepwise regression techniques to shortlist the number of antecedents of employee absenteeism* [Master's thesis, University of Twente] University of Twente Student Theses. https://essay.utwente.nl/74666/

Levine, R., Boniwell, I., Osin, E., & de Graaf, J. (2017). Time use and balance. In *Happiness: Transforming the Development Landscape*. The Centre for Bhutan Studies & GNH. (pp. 297–328). https://www.bhutanstudies.org.bt/publicationFiles/OccasionalPublications/Transforming%20Happiness/Happiness-transform_Final_with-cover.pdf

Pfeffer, J. (2018). *Dying for a paycheck: How modern management harms employee health and company performance—And what we can do about it*. Harper Business.

Ulmer, D. K., & Schwartzburd, L. (1996). Treatment of time pathologies. In R. Allan & S. S. Scheidt (Eds.), *Heart & mind: The practice of cardiac psychology* (pp. 329–362). American Psychological Association. https://doi.org/10.1037/10210-012

(page 8) Whole-time. This book and others in this collection encourage you to see your entire life and your perspective on time in this life, your personal story or narrative, as one seamless whole. The concept of *whole-time* means that every feature, detail, and nuance of your ongoing experience—your recollections of the past, your current state, your future imaginings and intentions—function as one single, unitary whole. The realization of whole-time both helps to reduce time urgency (see note above) and can be facilitated by visualizations of wholeness (e.g., mandala, map; see note below). The concept of whole-time has been studied in philosophy, psychology, and economics, with some examples provided here. In philosophy, an old essay by Leighton (1908) describes how the self can transcend time because we know we exist beyond only the present moment and understand that—by organizing spiritual meanings, purposes, and values—we experience a unity beyond time. More recently, studies of well-being indicate that we can take our entire life as a single project, attain a "balanced-time perspective" that aligns past, present, and future, and have a sense of our life as whole, purposeful, and satisfying (Şimşek, 2009). In economics, the concept of whole-time is used to show that the value of lost productive time among workers (due to injury) does not only pertain to work-related losses but to other reductions in the value that person provides (Krueger et al., 2001). In other words, time is not simply utilitarian and has meaning beyond productivity. This latter idea points to how modern economic forces and clock-time have led to a view of human beings as only having value through production and utility, thereby reducing our experience of whole-time.

Krueger, K. V., Ward, J. O., & Albrecht, G. R. (2001). Introduction to the whole-time concept. *Journal of Forensic Economics, 14*(1), 3–8. http://www.jstor.org/stable/42756072

Leighton, J. A. (1908). Time, change, and time-transcendence. *Journal of Philosophy, Psychology and Scientific Methods, 5*(21), 561–570. https://doi.org/10.2307/2010969

Şimşek, Ö. F. (2009). Happiness revisited: Ontological well-being as a theory-based construct of subjective well-being. *Journal of Happiness Studies, 10*(5), 505–522. https://doi.org/10.1007/S10902-008-9105-6

(page 9) About mandalas, map, tapestry, weave. As we evolve *in time*, insights emerge that no single image can accurately capture. Time is more a topography than a taxonomy. A map, weave, tapestry, and mandala are visualization devices. Cartographers create maps to help others journey. A tapestry helps us understand that the journey is made up of many layers and threads. A mandala is a symmetric or concentric spiritual symbol, a device for helping individuals see their place in life and in the cosmos. Access to different ways of visualizing allows us to shift perspective. The image shown on page iii is a map and a mandala. There is growing research on the use of mandala art therapy, where individuals draw or color images involving a symmetric and weaved pattern. Initial studies show that such drawing may help improve hopefulness in psychiatric patients (Kim et al., 2018), reduce anxiety in schoolchildren (Kostyunina & Drozdikova-Zaripova, 2016), and improve social functioning in autistic youth (Litchke et al., 2018).

Kim, H., Kim, S., Kwisoon, C., & Kim, J. (2018). Effects of mandala art therapy on subjective well-being, resilience, and hope in psychiatric inpatients. *Archives of Psychiatric Nursing, 32*(2), 167–173. https://doi.org/10.1016/j.apnu.2017.08.008

Kostyunina, N. Y., & Drozdikova-Zaripova, A. R. (2016). Adolescents' school anxiety correction by means of mandala art therapy. *International Journal of Environmental & Science Education, 11*(6), 1105–1116. https://files.eric.ed.gov/fulltext/EJ1114285.pdf

Litchke, L. G., Liu, T., & Castro, S. (2018). Effects of multimodal mandala yoga on social and emotional skills for youth with autism spectrum disorder: An exploratory study. *International Journal of Yoga, 11*(1), 59–65. https://pubmed.ncbi.nlm.nih.gov/29343932/

(page 10) Four Radiant Forces and time. I first proposed these Forces and the eight Trajectories in great detail and with supporting research in my book *Time and Intimacy: A New Science of Personal Relationships* (2000, Laurence Erlbaum Associates, Inc.). That book was written for an academic audience and for those studying intimacy in personal relationship research. Quest for Presence is in part an attempt to make these ideas more accessible to a wider audience. I describe these forces as part of a new language of time and sometimes reference research in quantum mechanics and cosmology to support claims about these forces. However, to be clear, the definition of time that we currently use as a human race (and across different cultures) and the definition of time in quantum mechanics, relativity theory, and cosmology refer to quite distinct levels of consciousness and reality. There are authors, some cited below, who attempt to weave a coherent framework or provide some way of drawing parallels and bridges between these levels. The purpose of Q*f*P is not to draw these parallels or propose some theory. Rather, I believe that human evolution has resulted in a very rich and multilayered definition of time for a reason (see Glossary). The definition will continue to evolve based on the transpersonal and spiritual insights we get from discussing our journey and sharing our insights about the four Forces and the ways they manifest (in the Attractions and Trajectories) and how they invite the development of our Soulful Capacities. For further reading on consciousness, time, and physics, consider these references below. There are also some great videos on time and quantum science on the PBS Nova series (https://www.pbs.org/wgbh/nova/), and Closer to Truth (https://www.closertotruth.com/).

Bohm, D. (2002). *Wholeness and the implicate order*. Routledge.

Greene, B. (2020). *Until the end of time: Mind, matter, and our search for meaning in an evolving universe*. Knopf.

Jeffery, K. J., & Rovelli, C. (2020). Transitions in brain evolution: Space, time and entropy. *Trends in Neurosciences, 43*(7), 467–474. https://doi.org/10.1016/j.tins.2020.04.008

Lanza, R., & Berman, B. (2016). *Beyond biocentrism: Rethinking time, space, consciousness, and the illusion of death*. BenBella Books, Inc.

Rovelli, C. (2018). *The order of time*. Riverhead Books.

Smolin, L. (2013). *Time reborn: From the crisis in physics to the future of the universe*. Houghton Mifflin Harcourt.

Wolf, F. A. (2004). *The yoga of time travel: How the mind can defeat time*. Quest Books.

CHAPTER 2

(page 30) For recent research on significant increase in the use of onsite stress-management programs, the Society for Human Resource Management (SHRM, 2019) reports a 5% to 13% increase from 2015 to 2019. For organizations that encourage stress management and report more positive health outcomes overall, see the 2018 report by the International Foundation of Employee Benefits Plans (IFEBP). For more organizations that are seeing stress and resilience programs as a "must have," see Schwartz et al. (2020). Readers can access the annual SHRM Benefits Surveys from their website. The links provided below were those used in research for this book.

International Foundation of Employee Benefits Plans. (2018). *Mental health and substance abuse benefits: 2018 survey results.* https://www.ifebp.org/store/Pages/Mental-Health-Survey.aspx

Schwartz, J., Mallon, D., Van Durme, Y., Hauptmann, M. Yan, R., & Poynton, S. (2020, May 15). *Beyond reskilling: Investing in resilience for uncertain futures.* Deloitte Insights. https://www2.deloitte.com/us/en/insights/focus/human-capital-trends/2020/reskilling-the-workforce-to-be-resilient.html

Society for Human Resource Management. (2019). *2019 employee benefits: U.S. employee benefits in 2019.* https://www.shrm.org/hr-today/trends-and-forecasting/research-and-surveys/pages/benefits19.aspx

I lived in Minnesota back in the early 1990s and would listen regularly to Wisconsin Public Radio's *Wisconsin Talks.* Sometime between 1990 and 1993, Jean Feraca interviewed the anthropologist Edward T. Hall. Despite a thorough search through program notes and tapes by the archivists at University Archives and Records Management at the University of Wisconsin-Madison, the episode with the interview has not been located and may not be available.

Hall, E. T. (1984). *The dance of life: The other dimension of time.* Anchor Books.

(page 33) Wellness champion research was documented in the following whitepaper. Simone, L., Bennett, J. B., Neeper, M., Linde, B., & Begley, K. (2017). *What champions do best: A special report for designed wellness champions.* ACEC Life/Health Trust. Also, see Bennett, J. B., & Linde, B. D. (2016). *Well-being champions: A competency-based guidebook.* Organizational Wellness & Learning Systems.

CHAPTER 3

(page 42) Brain maps and Karl Pribram. The study of the relationship between mapping time (i.e., our experience of it) and mapping the brain is beyond the scope of this book. There is experimental research on brain correlates of the specific sensation of time (e.g., Johnston & Nishida, 2001; Meck, 2005; Whittmann, 1999). More recently, research on brain activity with meditators who experience timelessness reveals insights into form. Berkovich-Ohana and colleagues (2013) discovered that the experience of timelessness involves specific brain frequencies (theta waves) in regions of the brain that relate to a sense of the body and alterations in regular body boundaries such that "the sense of self becomes diffused and 'spills out' of the body boundaries or simply disappears" (p. 16) This finding would be of interest to Karl Pribram, who saw the brain as encoded compressed forms of experience, whereby those forms we experience become attractors that guide us in navigating the world (Pribram, 2013). However, in moments of timelessness, our consciousness and experience transcend the body. Ultimately, a comprehensive map of time would account for all types of experiences and formulations of time, including those that transcend time altogether.

Berkovich-Ohana, A., Dor-Ziderman, Y., Glicksohn, J., & Goldstein, A. (2013). Alterations in the sense of time, space, and body in the mindfulness-trained brain: a neurophenomenologically-guided MEG study. *Frontiers in Psychology, 4*, Article 912. https://doi.org/10.3389/fpsyg.2013.00912

Johnston, A., & Nishida, S. (2001). Time perception: Brain time or event time? *Current Biology, 11*(11), R427–R430. https://doi.org/10.1016/S0960-9822(01)00252-4

Meck, W. H. (2005). Neuropsychology of timing and time perception. *Brain and Cognition, 58*(1), 1–8. https://doi.org/10.1016/j.bandc.2004.09.004

Pribram, K. H. (2013). *The form within: My point of view.* Prospecta Press.

Wittmann, M. (1999). Time perception and temporal processing levels of the brain. *Chronobiology International, 16*(1), 17–32. https://doi.org/10.3109/07420529908998709

(page 47) The Spiritual Enneagram or Holy Ideas. These ideas were originally developed by Oscar Ichazo in his work with the Arica School. Books 2 and 3 in Quest for Presence also describe aspects of the Enneagram. Briefly, the Enneagram is a nine-pointed teaching system, framework, or model for understanding the difference between spiritual aspects of our human nature (soul or essence) and other aspects that lead to pain and suffering (ego, attachment, personality fixations). The Holy Ideas are a core aspect of study that, when contemplated and understood, help us to get in touch with our spiritual nature. The Nine Holy Ideas are Holy Perfection, Holy Will, Holy Harmony, Holy Origin, Holy Omniscience, Holy Faith, Holy Wisdom, Holy Truth and Holy Love. Before reading the references below, I encourage students to visit the Arica School of Knowledge website and participate in an experiential training. See https://www.arica.org/

Almaas, A. H. (2000). *Facets of unity: The Enneagram of holy ideas.* Shambhala Publications.

Howell, J. B. (2012). *Becoming conscious: The Enneagram's forgotten passageway.* Balboa Press.

Maitri, S. (2000). *The spiritual dimension of the Enneagram: Nine faces of the soul.* Jeremy P. Tarcher/Putnam.

CHAPTER 4

(page 57) More time with technology than with others. There is a relationship between increased use of smartphones and the internet and less time interacting with others. The relationship is complex and depends upon age, use of social media, and time spent in other leisure activities, particularly watching television. Research in this area continues to grow and evolve to reveal important variations. A sampling of studies is provided below that suggests we spend less time having deeper conversations (McPherson et al., 2006), that smartphone addiction is driven by lack of social support (Herrero et al., 2019), and that people are spending increasing amounts of time on social media. And 46% say they spend more time on their cell phone than with their significant other. (Wheelwright, 2022).

Broadband Search. (2022). *Average time spent daily on social media (Latest 2022 data)*. https://www.broadbandsearch.net/blog/average-daily-time-on-social-media

Herrero, J., Torres, A., Vivas, P., & Urueña, A. (2019). Smartphone addiction and social support: A three-year longitudinal study. *Psychosocial Intervention, 28*(3), 111–118. https://doi.org/10.5093/pi2019a6

Kemp, S. (2019, January 30). *Digital trends 2019: Every single stat you need to know about the internet*. TNW. https://thenextweb.com/news/digital-trends-2019-every-single-stat-you-need-to-know-about-the-internet

McPherson, M., Smith-Lovin, L., & Brashears, M. E. (2006). Social isolation in America: Changes in core discussion networks over two decades. *American Sociological Review, 71*(3), 353–375. https://doi.org/10.1177/000312240607100301

Wheelwright, T. (2022). *2022 cell phone usage statistics: How obsessed are we?* Reviews.org. https://www.reviews.org/mobile/cell-phone-addiction/#Smart_Phone_Addiction_Stats

CHAPTER 5

(page 70) Brain default mode. This is generally defined as the level of neuronal activity when people are in an awake resting state with no goal-directed activity (no strong task constraints) and generally with eyes closed. It appears that even in this state, those parts of the brain remain active that are responsible for continual scanning the environment, gathering, and evaluating information. This is sometimes discussed as mind wandering. Some claim that this default mode network (DMN) overlaps greatly with brain areas responsible for social cognition, thinking about and mapping relationships we have with others, and our place within our social network. For our quest for presence work, DMN regions are sometimes associated with maladaptive mind wandering and susceptibility to negative mood states.

Hove, M. J., Stelzer, J., Nierhaus, T., Thiel, S. D., Gundlach, C., Margulies, D. S., Van Dijk, K. R. A., Turner, R., Keller, P. E., & Merker, B. (2016). Brain network reconfiguration and perceptual decoupling during an absorptive state of consciousness. *Cerebral Cortex, 26*(7), 3116–3124. https://doi.org/10.1093/cercor/bhv137

Mars, R. B., Neubert, F. X., Noonan, M. P., Sallet, J., Toni, I., & Rushworth, M. F. S. (2012). On the relationship between the "default mode network" and the "social brain." *Frontiers in Human Neuroscience, 6*, Article 189. https://doi.org/10.3389/fnhum.2012.00189

Raichle, M. E., MacLeod, A. M., Snyder, A. Z., Powers, W. J., Gusnard, D. A., & Shulman, G. L. (2001). A default mode of brain function. *Proceedings of the National Academy of Sciences, 98*(2), 676–682. https://doi.org/10.1073/pnas.98.2.676

(page 71) Decline in mental functions, aging, and experience of time. Research suggests that mental decline in aging and dementia is associated with more attunement to the experience of different dimensions of time (Eriksen et al., 2020). The ability to remember to plan, initiate, carry out, and complete future intentions (e.g., remembering to attend an appointment) are referred to as prospective memory (PM) in the research literature. While PM clearly declines with age, it can be slowed down with certain supports. Other studies show that dementia is associated with the experience of time slowing down and less time pressure. Clearly, a new and different experience of time emerges as brain function declines and the mental processes they serve also fade. It is possible that if the four specific processes (memory, intention, attention, and labeling) have specific relationships to the deeper cosmological forces, then in very old age (senescence), we get more in touch with these deeper and raw aspects of time ("lived time") and let go of artificial clock-time.

Craik, F. I. M., & Kerr, S. A. (1995). Commentary: Prospective memory, aging, and lapses of intention. In M. Brandimonte, G. O. Einstein, & M. A. McDaniel (Eds.), *Prospective memory: Theory and applications* (pp. 227–237). Lawrence Erlbaum Associates.

Eriksen, S., Bartlett, R. L., Grov, E. K., Ibsen, T. L., Telenius, E. W., & Mork Rokstad, A. M. (2020). The experience of lived time in people with dementia: A systematic meta-synthesis. *Dementia and Geriatric Cognitive Disorders, 49*(5), 435–455. https://doi.org/10.1159/000511225

Haines, S., Shelton, J., Henry, J., Terrett, G., Vorwerk, T., and Rendell, P. (2019). Prospective memory and cognitive aging. *Oxford Research Encyclopedia of Psychology.* https://doi.org/10.1093/acrefore/9780190236557.013.381

Rummel, J., & McDaniel, M. A. (Eds.). (2019). *Prospective memory.* Routledge.

Torboli, D., Mioni, G., Bussé, C., Cagnin, A., & Vallesi, A. (2021). Subjective experience of time in dementia with Lewy bodies during COVID-19 lockdown. *Current Psychology.* https://doi.org/10.1007/s12144-021-01811-7

(page 75) Research on suicide and suicide prevention is a growing and dynamic field. Here is just a sample of articles. Key takeaways from some of these studies are that interventions may be more effective when individuals receive one-on-one attention to their individual characteristics and when various aspects of the community (healthcare, schools, hospitals) are involved and interconnected in their support. If you are concerned about suicidal risk in yourself or others, please reach out for help. In the United States, please contact the 988 Suicide & Crisis Lifeline by dialing (or SMS) 988 or visit https://988lifeline.org/.

Doupnik, S. K., Rudd, B., Schmutte, T., Worsley, D., Bowden, C. F., McCarthy, E., Eggan, E., Bridge, J. A., & Marcus, S. C. (2020). Association of suicide prevention interventions with subsequent suicide attempts, linkage to follow-up care, and depression symptoms for acute care settings: A systematic review and meta-analysis. *JAMA Psychiatry, 77*(10), 1021–1030. https://doi.org/10.1001/jamapsychiatry.2020.1586

Hofstra, E., van Nieuwenhuizen, C., Bakker, M., Özgül, D., Elfeddali, I., de Jong, S. J., & van der Feltz-Cornelis, C. M. (2020). Effectiveness of suicide prevention interventions: A systematic review and meta-analysis. *General Hospital Psychiatry, 63*, 127–140. https://doi.org/10.1016/j.genhosppsych.2019.04.011

Howarth, E. J., O'Connor, D. B., Panagioti, M., Hodkinson, A., Wilding, S., & Johnson, J. (2020). Are stressful life events prospectively associated with increased suicidal ideation and behaviour? A systematic review and meta-analysis. *Journal of Affective Disorders, 266*, 731–742. https://doi.org/10.1016/j.jad.2020.01.171

Klonsky, E. D., May, A. M., & Saffer, B. Y. (2016). Suicide, suicide attempts, and s uicidal ideation. *Annual Review of Clinical Psychology, 12*, 307–330. https://doi.org/10.1146/annurev-clinpsy-021815-093204

(page 80) We downplay the influence of others and the situation on our behavior. A broad field of research on social cognition strongly indicates the prevalence of self-serving and inaccurate biases (e.g., stereotypes, implicit bias) on perception of self and others. Human beings sacrifice accuracy when compelled to protect, heal, maintain, or enhance a sense of self. The "fundamental attribution error" is one of the most studied and refers to the overall tendency to attribute the behavior of others (especially mistakes and failure) to their character or traits rather than the equally plausible influence of the surrounding situation or context. A recent meta-analysis suggests that biases that support self-enhancement are more beneficial for personal adjustment than for relationships and getting along with others. See Dufner, M., Gebauer, J. E., Sedikides, C., & Denissen, J. J. A. (2019). Self-enhancement and psychological adjustment: A meta-analytic review. *Personality and Social Psychology Review, 23*(1), 48–72. https://doi.org/10.1177/1088868318756467

(page 80) Self-awareness. Efforts to correct bias and enhance self-awareness are growing. These two references point to both research and methods.

Eurich, T. (2017). *Insight: The surprising truth about how others see us, how we see ourselves, and why the answers matter more than we think.* Currency. See also http://www.insight-book.com/

Fernández-Sotos, P., Torio, I., Fernández-Caballero, A., Navarro, E., González, P., Dompablo, M., & Rodriguez-Jimenez, R. (2019). Social cognition remediation interventions: A systematic mapping review. *PLoS ONE, 14*(6), Article e0218720. https://doi.org/10.1371/journal.pone.0218720

(page 82) Deepak Chopra quotation is from Chopra, D. (2006). *Power, freedom, and grace: Living from the source of lasting happiness.* Amber-Allen Publishing.

(page 84) "Life expectancy" calculators are available on the internet. As part of this exercise, you may explore them. Keep in mind that they are only estimates and subject to error and change. It is best to take several and to do so every few months. Research shows that none of the estimators has been actually validated.

Life Expectancy Calculators: https://www.lifeexpectancycalculators.com/statistical-lifespan/

Project Big Life (Canada): https://www.projectbiglife.ca/life-expectancy-calculator

Social Security Administration (US): https://www.ssa.gov/oact/population/longevity.html

(page 84) For research on estimators, see Rector, T., Taylor, B., Sultan, S., Shaukat, A., Adabag, S., Nelson, D., Capecchi, T., MacDonald, R., Greer, N., & Wilt, T. (2016, June). *Life expectancy calculators.* Department of Veterans Affairs (U.S.). https://www.ncbi.nlm.nih.gov/books/NBK424560/

(page 86) Totality of reality and the sacred hoop. There are a number of books that some may consider "New Age" revisionist writings of Native American philosophy about the nature of the world and the interconnectedness of all things. This small sample of writings provides a starting point for interested readers.

Brooks, K. P. (2014). *Sacred relationships: Psychology for the soul.* Xlibris.

Dyer, D. (2020). *The return of collective intelligence: Ancient wisdom for a world out of balance.* Bear & Company.

Forbes, J. D. (2001). Indigenous Americans: Spirituality and ecos. *Daedalus, 130*(4), 283–300. https://www.jstor.org/stable/20027728

Mazzola, L. C. (1988). The medicine wheel: Center and periphery. *The Journal of Popular Culture, 22*(2), 63–73. https://doi.org/10.1111/j.0022-3840.1988.2202_63.x

CHAPTER 6

(page 90) Quote by Don Lincoln. Lincoln. D. (2013, August 5). *The good vibrations of quantum field theories.* NOVA Newsletter. https://www.pbs.org/wgbh/nova/article/the-good-vibrations-of-quantum-field-theories/

(page 90) **The "overview" effect** experienced by astronauts has been subject to some systematic study. The seminal book is White, F. (1998). *The overview effect: Space exploration and human evolution.* AIAA (American Institute of Aeronautics & Astronautics); which more recently published White, F. (2019). *The cosma hypothesis: Implications of the overview effect.* Independently Published. Listen to a NASA podcast with White: https://www.nasa.gov/johnson/HWHAP/the-overview-effect. Here is the Wikipedia page https://en.wikipedia.org/wiki/Overview_effect. Other example studies are listed below.

Voski, A. (2020). The ecological significance of the overview effect: Environmental attitudes and behaviours in astronauts. *Journal of Environmental Psychology, 70,* Article 101454. https://doi.org/10.1016/j.jenvp.2020.101454

Yaden, D. B., Iwry, J., Slack, K. J., Eichstaedt, J. C., Zhao, Y., Vaillant, G. E., & Newberg, A. B. (2016). The overview effect: Awe and self-transcendent experience in space flight. *Psychology of Consciousness: Theory, Research, and Practice, 3*(1), 1–11. https://doi.org/10.1037/cns0000086

Perhaps the most widely read book on the subject is Carl Sagan's (1994) *Pale blue dot: A vision of the human future in space.* Random House Publishing Group.

(page 90) **Hubble telescope.** I recommend taking time, on a routine basis, to view images from the Hubble telescope, which, as of 2020, has been in orbit for thirty years. You can find them at https://www.nasa.gov/mission_pages/hubble/main/index.html. Also, check out the James Webb Space Telescope at https://webb.nasa.gov/.

(page 91) **The universe is itself a matrix of energy,** much like a weave of information. The ostensible science behind this idea (string theory, unified field theory) is subject to debate as baseless philosophy, despite the extensive amount of writing about it. Below are some examples. The initial idea that the universe functions like an informational hologram may be attributed to David Bohm. The use of the term "totality" is similar to Bohm's use of the term "plenum" as one, seamless, unbroken background of energy that fills all the universe.

Braden, G. (2008). *The divine matrix: Bridging time, space, miracles, and belief* (1st ed.). Hay House Inc.

Currivan, J. (2017). *The cosmic hologram: In-formation at the center of creation.* Inner Traditions.

Kuhn, R. L. (2015, May 23). *Forget space-time: Information may create the cosmos.* Space.com. https://www.space.com/29477-did-information-create-the-cosmos.html

Lanza, R. (2016). *Beyond biocentrism: Rethinking time, space, consciousness, and the illusion of death.* BenBella Books.

Nichol, L. (Ed.). (2002). *The essential David Bohm*. Routledge.

(page 94) The forces work in a homeostatic way. I do not have any proof for this but I hypothesize that the forces represent a living universe, one that is continually breathing and, like all life, functions to survive and thrive through homeostasis. A simple definition of homeostasis is a self-regulating process by which a living system acts (Time Shapes) to maintain stability (Form) while adjusting to ongoing conditions and perturbations (Chaos) that are optimal for growth and becoming (Nurturing Conditions). Book 4 in Q*f*P also explains how the eight Trajectories work in a homeostatic, self-regulating, relationship to each other. In that book, the trajectory of Pace is especially defined by and through homeostasis. Homeostasis may also be the basis for consciousness (see Book 3) and interested readers may wish to study the writing of neuroscientist Damasio, A. (2021). *Feeling & knowing: Making minds conscious*. Pantheon Books.

(page 96) The correspondences with Contemplation Q*f*P 1-6 exercise are: (1) Gravity relates to statement 2 (We have a responsibility to organize our lives … A place for everything and everything in its place); (2) Entropy relates to statement 1 (There will always be mystery … Life innovates, has a wildness to it …); (3) Cause and Effect relates to statement 4 (Taking action, achieving results … Carpe Diem); and (4) Self-organizing relates to statement 3 (Everything is shaping up … To everything there is a season).

CHAPTER 8

(page 104) We coregulate our lives together. The work of Stephen Porges on polyvagal theory claims that the human nervous system is a fundamentally social system, that human beings cannot evolve and navigate the world without developing apparatus for social communication, for regulating and conveying emotions through such communication, and for experiencing the wide range of possible feelings that make up a healthy human experience of life.

Porges, S. W. (2011). *The polyvagal theory: Neurophysiological foundations of emotions, attachment, communication, and self-regulation (Norton series on interpersonal neurobiology)*. W. W. Norton & Company.

Dana, D. (2018). *The polyvagal theory in therapy: Engaging the rhythm of regulation (Norton series on interpersonal neurobiology)*. W. W. Norton & Company.

CHAPTER 9

(pages 113–117) Wisdom. There is a growing research literature on the study of wisdom and its relationship to the experience of time. The Canadian psychologist Jeffrey Dean Webster is currently one of the leading scientists in the study of wisdom. In one study (Webster et al., 2014), he and colleagues assessed both a measure of wisdom and a measure of "balanced time perspective." The strong relationship between these measures led the authors to conclude that "Wise persons learn from their past, and reminisce in order to regulate emotions, and resolve (or work on) challenging or traumatic events from earlier in life. Wise persons also recognize the positive motivational consequences of setting long-term goals and nurture an optimistic and expansive future orientation." Other references are provided that explore the relationship between time and wisdom. Together, they suggest wisdom is closely tied to an appreciation of temporal context (e.g., life review and seeing how different factors, forces, or features of life weave together).

Brown, S. C., & Greene, J. A. (2006). The wisdom development scale: Translating the conceptual to the concrete. *Journal of College Student Development*, 47(1), 1–19. https://doi.org/10.1353/csd.2006.0002

Glück, J., König, S., Naschenweng, K., Redzanowski, U., Dorner, L., Straßer, I., & Wiedermann, W. (2013). How to measure wisdom: Content, reliability, and validity of five measures. *Frontiers in Psychology*, 4, Article 405. https://psycnet.apa.org/doi/10.3389/fpsyg.2013.00405

Jeste, D. V., Ardelt, M., Blazer, D., Kraemer, H. C., Vaillant, G., & Meeks, T. W. (2010). Expert consensus on characteristics of wisdom: A Delphi method study. *The Gerontologist, 50*(5), 668–680. https://doi.org/10.1093/geront/gnq022

Webster, J. D., Bohlmeijer, E. T., & Westerhof, G. J. (2014). Time to flourish: The relationship of temporal perspective to well-being and wisdom across adulthood. *Aging & Mental Health, 18*(8), 1046–1056. https://doi.org/10.1080/13607863.2014.908458

Readers interested in the process of self-transcendence may wish to read Book 2 of QfP. In particular, I discuss how the concept of soul in modern psychological science has evolved from its more spiritual origins into a psychological construct. This is partly due to how Maslow's work has been misrepresented in textbooks in psychology. See Koltko-Rivera (2006).

Koltko-Rivera, M. E. (2006). Rediscovering the later version of Maslow's hierarchy of needs: Self-transcendence and opportunities for theory, research, and unification. *Review of general psychology, 10*(4), 302–317. https://psycnet.apa.org/doi/10.1037/1089-2680.10.4.302

ADDITIONAL TREASURE REFERENCES

(pages 136–137) There are many examples of the treasures we experience in life that come from the arts, literature, and religious texts. This includes the use of the terms *treasure* and *treasure in heaven* in the Bible and a source text in the third century religion Manichaesim titled "The Treasures of Life." A full description of these is beyond the scope of this book and even of Book 5, which is dedicated to the Treasures. The references for the Treasures listed in the appendix are included here:

Brussat, F., & Brussat, M. A. (1998). *Spiritual literacy: Reading the sacred in everyday life*. Simon and Schuster.

Kaplan, C. (2004). *The invisible garment: 30 spiritual principles that weave the fabric of human life*. Jodere Group.

Maslow, A. (1970). *Religions, values, and peak experiences*. Penguin Books.

READINGS ON TIME BEYOND TIME

(pages 138–140) The five selected readings in this section are not meant to be exhaustive or representative of the vast array of spiritual and religious texts that treat the subject of time from a spiritual perspective. In some cases, I have adapted or shortened the language from the original text but hope to have preserved the core meaning.

Johnson, C. (2014). *A better life: 100 atheists speak out on joy & meaning in a world without god*. Cosmic Teapot, Inc.

The diamond sutra and the sutra of Hui-Neng. (A. F. Price, & W. Mou-lam Trans.). (1993). In J. Kornfield (Ed.), *Teachings of the Buddha* (p. 143). Shambhala Publications.

The Holy Bible: English Standard Version. (2001). Crossway.

The Holy Bible: New International Version. (1984). Grand Rapid.

The Holy Qur'an. (A.Y. Ali, Trans.). (2001). Wordsworth.

Acknowledgments

This is the tale of two journeys: My own story and also the story of the Quest for Presence itself. Throughout the books in the Q*f*P collection, I acknowledge many teachers, friends, and family for their contribution to my story. For those personal acknowledgements, I direct readers to the books, especially Chapter 7 in Book 3.

But the story of this entire collection—the many who helped birth it, and its many phases—all began with several opportunities to share early ideas. Thanks to Dr. Steve Duck, Lawrence Erlbaum Press published *Time and Intimacy: A New Science of Personal Relationships* in 2000. These were research and academic ideas. I yearned to have more practical conversations and started searching. I was first graced with the open arms of the C. G. Jung Society of North Texas (thank you, Maureen Lumley), Unity Church of Dallas and also of Fort Worth, Magellan Healthcare, and also Brandeis University (thank you, Marci McPhee), all of whom brought me in to conduct workshops or retreats in 2000 and early 2001. These offerings had titles like "The Quest for Presence: Time & the Transformation of Work," "Time & Intimacy: Finding Serenity in a Busy World," and "Time and the Soul's Journey." Positive reactions from many participants suggested my ideas had personal relevance.

Around that time, I sent a copy of *Time and Intimacy* to the then-editor of *Spirituality & Health* magazine, Stephen Kiesling. Steve was a key to everything that came next. Through several great conversations, he helped me to reimagine my early drafts of the Quest for Presence Inventory™ (QFPI™). Thanks to Steve for publishing "Navigating in Time" in his magazine in the Winter 2002 issue. I received some calls from readers of that article. One, in particular, was a bookstore owner who encouraged me to write a book.

I also continued to offer workshops, especially at the National Wellness Institute (NWI) in Stevens Point, Wisconsin. I also delivered a train-the-trainer workshop at NWI on "Time and Spiritual Health." Then, the Center for Substance Abuse Prevention (CSAP) at the Substance Abuse and Mental Health Services Administration (SAMHSA) provided further support. Because of a CSAP research grant, between 2002 and 2004 I was able to deliver "Time and Spiritual Health" to employees at small businesses in the Dallas-Fort Worth Metroplex as part of a randomized clinical trial. I especially want to thank Dr. Deborah Galvin, who helped me navigate the grant application and implementation process.

This research study made the concepts even more real. My colleagues (from the Recovery Resource Council in Fort Worth) and I taught "Time and Spiritual Health" to employees in diverse occupations, including car wash attendants, construction workers, engineers, employees in a manufacturing plant, school bus drivers, university administrators, teachers, and physical plant staff. When results from our research with these "everyday" people showed improvements in well-being, I knew these ideas were no longer just academic concepts. Thanks to Richard Sledz, Camille Patterson, Kelly Heath, Wyndy Wiitala and the whole team who helped to implement this study. Thanks to Shawn Reynolds for getting these research findings published.

The many conversations with dozens of these early colleagues and students laid the foundation for the next phase of this work. I am grateful to them and apologize for not mentioning them all. This next phase began with writing. The first draft of *Quest for Presence* was actually a single book. I asked Sandra Wendel (of Write On, Inc.), the editor for my previous book, *Raw Coping Power: From Stress to Thriving,* to start editing. Instead, Sandy suggested I first have a group of beta readers provide feedback. She recommended approaching individuals who were familiar with my work as well as others who did not know me.

This five-book Quest for Presence collection emerged as a result of the in-depth, honest, and very insightful feedback from twenty beta readers. Sandy received the feedback anonymously but separately shared the names of reviewers. I am grateful to Sandy for her ongoing guidance (then and now) and to each and every one of the reviewers: Art Wimberly, Briane Agostinelli, Cassie Menn, Cynthia Conigliaro, Gary Loper, Heather Sittler, Heidi Postupack, Janette Helm, Jaymee Spannring, Katharine Hunter, Kimberly Gray, Laura Crowder, Michele Studer, Paul Feather, Rachel Kopke, Regina Novak, Rose Whitcomb, Sadie Liller, Sandy Kogut, and Teresa Przetocki. I also appreciate input from Faith Geiger, Rachael Baker, Janet DeLong and many others who I likely have forgotten. Oh, Wait! Special thanks to Kimberly Gray for always reminding me about the quantum "popping in."

These reviewers were given a list of almost 20 questions, providing a structure for their reactions to the book. Nonetheless, I was overwhelmed with the sheer amount and detail of feedback—almost 20,000 words and over 40 pages. My colleague Shelby Pittman combed through the data searching for common words and themes. Her analysis revealed that readers were excited about the content but overwhelmed by the complexity and depth of the ideas. Importantly, they wanted to retain all the key features of the book; for example, the spiritual message, the odes, the contemplations, and my own story. Many suggested that several books and a separate workbook would make the quest easier to digest. Shelby helped me take the next step to start restructuring the book.

At the same time, I had started teaching virtual courses of "The Quest for Presence." The students who took the class also helped me further refine ideas, and several contributed their QFPI™ profiles (see Book 3). These students included Anissa Amason, Briane Agostinelli, Laura Anne Crowder, Cynthia Conigliaro, Tracey Cox, Madge Cruse, Tyler Currier, Melanie DuPon, Shahinaz Elhennawi, Kristie Ellison, Brenda Fister, Kimberly Gray, Deborah Hamlin, Susan Hansen, Mark Head, Lucy Hoblitzelle, Kathleen Klug, Lindsay Levin, Michele Mariscal, Jennifer Markley, Jocelyne Maurice, Wesley Miller, Renee Moy,

Alan Porzio, Sazha Ramos, Desiree Reynolds, Sandy Salvo, John Shelton, Stephany Sherry, Andy Siegle, John Steakley, Michele Studer, Zac Tolbert, Melanie Weinberger, Art Wimberly, and Susan Yenzer. Thank you for your presence.

Throughout this process, I have been most grateful to those contributing a "treasure story" (see Book 1 and Book 5). This includes a number of people already mentioned, as well as Kathy Carlton, Sara Christopher (Acker), Michaela Conley, and John Weaver. Thank you for reminding me that the treasures are real and true.

Repackaging a single document into a collection and workbook was daunting. I want to thank Shelby again for her help. Also, Aldrich Chan went through manuscripts, collated all the research references, and found the proper citations for the hundreds of research notes found at the back of every book. Both Shelby's and Aldrich's responsiveness to my requests was a tremendous aid that kept me going.

The final phase of this story was guided by my editors. First, thanks to Sue Hansen of Duck Sauce Life for her exquisite detail in meaningful developmental reviews. Sue's questions, along with her own personal insights, helped me to further clarify ideas in substantive rewrites. Candace Johnson took these edited drafts and, with great thoughtfulness, helped to refine final drafts. Thank you, Sue and Candace, for your patient and thorough work.

Special thanks go to others who helped with design: Gary Rosenberg (from The Book Couple) for beautiful interior design and book cover, Jeffrey McQuirk for his ideas and patience in rendering the images of the four radiant forces, and my dear friend Ellen McCown for her gentle spirit and suggestions for artwork.

At the start of this acknowledgment section, I refer readers to reading the books to find acknowledgments of people in my personal life. I also have to give special thanks to my friends Art Wimberly, Spencer Seidman, and Cynthia Conigliaro—each of whom spent many hours listening to me ramble on and on about my struggles as a writer on this quest of time. Their playful feedback helped me feel so much less alone during periods of dismay and doubt. Thanks, guys!

Finally, I could say that none of this would have been possible without the love, support, and kindest patience of my wife, Jan. The truth is, I could have pulled off some of it ... maybe. However, I know it would not be anything approaching the rich tapestry that I hope readers see through so many words. My own ability to see this tapestry—of the preciousness of this life and my love of life—comes from Jan. She, more than anyone I have ever known, lightens me, gives me confidence, and so makes it possible for me to listen more and listen deeply. I am so grateful to her and our many years together.

About the Author

Joel Bennett, PhD, is president of Organizational Wellness & Learning Systems (OWLS), a consulting firm that specializes in evidence-based wellness and e-learning technologies to promote organizational health and employee well-being. Dr. Bennett first delivered stress management programming in 1985, and through the efforts of over 400 resilience facilitators and coaches who have been trained in OWLS' evidence-informed curriculum as well as consulting in South Africa, Italy, and Brazil, OWLS programs have since reached over 250,000 workers across the United States and internationally. OWLS has received over $6 million in National Institutes of Health funding for workplace well-being research, and their programs have been recognized as effective by independent bodies, including the US Surgeon General.

OWLS consults on Integral Organizational Wellness™ approaches that combine leadership, champion, team, and peer-to-peer strategies: nudging the true culture of health. Joel is the author of 50 peer-reviewed research articles and chapters and has authored or coauthored eight books, including *Heart-Centered Leadership* (with Susan Steinbrecher), *Raw Coping Power: From Stress to Thriving, Your Best Self at Work* (with Ben Dilla), *Well-Being Champions: A Competency-Based Guidebook, Time and Intimacy, Preventing Workplace Substance Abuse,* and *The Connoisseur of Time.*

Dr. Bennett has served in advisory and board roles for various organizations including Magellan Health; Aetna; the National Wellness Institute; It's Time Texas, Work Healthier Advisory Committee; the Academy of Management Division on Management and

Spirituality; the Global Wellness Institute; the International Foundation of Employee Benefits Plans; and the State of Texas Primary Prevention Planning Committee (Preventing Sexual Violence).

In 2022, he received the William B. Baun Lifetime Achievement Award from the National Wellness Institute for his contributions to the professional field of wellness. He also received the Positive Leadership Award from the Positive Leadership Institute for forward-thinking management practices that help employees, teams, and organizations thrive.

Joel lives in North Texas with Jan, his wife of twenty-eight years, and around the corner from his wonderful son, daughter-in-law, and grandchildren, who call him "Obi." He hopes that one day he will become a Jedi Knight or something.

Made in the USA
Coppell, TX
16 March 2023

14313538R10103